Miners' Battalion

Miners' Battalion

A History of the 12th (Pioneers) King's Own Yorkshire Light Infantry 1914–1918

Captain R. Ede England

Edited by Malcolm K. Johnson

Pen & Sword
MILITARY

First published in Great Britain in 2017 by
Pen & Sword Military
an imprint of
Pen & Sword Books Ltd
47 Church Street
Barnsley
South Yorkshire
S70 2AS

ISBN 978 1 47386 808 3

A CIP catalogue record for this book is available from the British
Library

Typeset in Ehrhardt by
Mac Style Ltd, Bridlington, East Yorkshire
Printed and bound in the UK by CPI Group (UK) Ltd,
Croydon, CR0 4YY

Pen & Sword Books Ltd incorporates the imprints of Pen & Sword
Archaeology, Atlas, Aviation, Battleground, Discovery, Family
History, History, Maritime, Military, Naval, Politics, Railways, Select,
Transport, True Crime, Fiction, Frontline Books, Leo Cooper,
Praetorian Press, Seaforth Publishing and Wharncliffe.

For a complete list of Pen & Sword titles please contact
PEN & SWORD BOOKS LIMITED
47 Church Street, Barnsley, South Yorkshire, S70 2AS, England
E-mail: enquiries@pen-and-sword.co.uk
Website: www.pen-and-sword.co.uk

Lieutenant Colonel R.C. Dill

Enlisted in the 7th Dragoon Guards in June 1881, and went to Egypt as a trooper in 1882. Was present at the Battle of Tell-El-Kebir and holds the Khedive's Star and the Egyptian Medal with bar. In 1883 he proceeded to India and in June 1886, was awarded a commission in the Wiltshire Regiment. Was promoted to the rank of Captain in the King's Own Yorkshire Light Infantry in 1895, and served through the South African War from 1899 to 1902, where he was wounded and mentioned in Dispatches for gallantry in action. Promoted Major in the 5th Fusiliers in 1901, he retired from the Army in 1904 under the age clause. In 1906 he was appointed Brigade Major of Volunteers (afterwards transformed into the Territorial Army) which appointment he held for five years. On the outbreak of the Great War in 1914, he took command of the 9th Battalion King's Own Yorkshire Light Infantry, and was later transferred to command of the 12th Battalion of the same Regiment, with the rank of Lieutenant Colonel. Owing to a breakdown in health, caused very largely by his South African wound, he resigned this command on 19 May 1915, and in 1916 was appointed Assistant Recruiting Officer at Exeter. Here he remained for almost two years when bad health again cut short his activities and in 1918 he was pronounced unfit for further service.

Those whom this book commemorates were numbered among those who at the call of the King and Country left all that was dear to them, enduring hardship, faced danger, and finally passed out of the sight of men by the path of duty and self-sacrifice, giving up their own lives that others might live in freedom. Let those who come after see to it that their names be not forgotten.

TO THE MEMORY OF THE
Officers, Non-Commissioned Officers and Men
Of the

12th Battalion King's Own Yorkshire Light Infantry

(Miners, Pioneers)

Who gave their lives in the cause of
Freedom during the Great War

1914–1918

THIS BOOK IS DEDICATED

Contents

Foreword

The King's Own Yorkshire Light Infantry has a long distinguished record of service in the past, of which the Regiment is justly proud. The new units raised for the Great War imbibed readily the spirit of their senior Battalions and none did more to emulate their predecessors than the 12th Battalion, whose deeds are so accurately and interestingly told in this book.

The initial training the Battalion received laid the foundation of that spirit of discipline and self-sacrifice for which it was noted, whether serving with the Division or detached for special duty. When sent to Flanders for the Third Battle of Ypres their services were the subject of highly complimentary reports from the Corps and Army Commanders.

Major General Wanless O'Gowan, General Officer Commanding 31st Division from August 1915–20 March 1918.

Having been associated with the Battalion for over two and a half years, I am glad to be given the opportunity of paying a tribute to the Officers, NCO's and Men who did so much for the honour and welfare of the 31st Division.

R. Wanless O'Gowan, Major-General
Late Commanding 31st Division.

Acknowledgements

The first person to be acknowledged in this reproduction of the history of the 12th King's Own Yorkshire Light Infantry 1914–1918 must be the original author, Captain R. Ede England. His intimate knowledge of this Battalion allowed him to describe in detail the part it played during the war and the difficulties experienced by these former miners and engineers who found themselves caught up in the world's first truly industrialized global war.

The photographs included in the book were all taken by one or more members of the battalion, despite the fact that Army Regulations forbade the use of cameras at the front. Many of the photographs are from the collection held in the archive of the King's Own Yorkshire Light Infantry Museum, which is located in Doncaster Museum, and I must thank Steve Tagg, a member of the Museum staff, for retrieving them from the Regiment's huge collection of photographs. Other photographs were kindly loaned by Michael Wood and Mary Palmer whose ancestors, Private George Barber Wood and Lance Corporal William Davis both served with 12th KOYI. The photographs including Major D.E. Roberts were kindly provided by his niece Mrs Ruth Strong and her daughter Rachael. It is unfortunate that so few of the men in these photographs could be identified.

Rayna Ryley, of the Wakefield Library was kind enough to help fill in some of the gaps of missing photographs in the Regiment's copy of the original book. Mathew Thomas, also of the Wakefield Library, was instrumental in putting me in touch with Neal Rigby, a former member of staff at Queen Elizabeth's Grammar School Wakefield and Elaine Merckx, a current member of staff who provided the background information concerning Captain England.

I must also thank Major Andrew Penny, chairman of the Trustees of the King's Own Yorkshire Light Infantry Regimental Museum, for allowing me full access to the Regimental Archive, and a prolonged loan of Captain England's original book. Finally, I must thank my wife Wendy for once more patiently reading, checking and correcting the early drafts of this book.

Malcolm K. Johnson
2017

List of Maps

Abbreviations

ASC	Army Service Corps
BEF	British Expeditionary Force
CB	Companion of the Order of the Bath
CBE	Commander Brigade Engineers
C-in-C	Commander in Chief
CO	Commanding Officer
Coy	Company
CRA	Commander Royal Artillery
CRE	Commander Royal Engineers
CSM	Company Sergeant Major
DADOS	Deputy Assistant Director of Ordnance Supplies
DAH	Disordered action of the heart
DAQMG	Deputy Assistant Quartermaster General
DCM	Distinguished Conduct Medal
DSO	Distinguished Service order
GCVO	Grand Cross of the Victorian Order
GHQ	General Headquarters
GOC	General Officer Commanding
GSW	General Service Waggon
HMT	His Majesty's Transporter (Troopship)
KCB	Knight Commander of the Bath
KCB	Knight Grand Cross of the Order of the Bath
KCMG	Knight Commander of the Order of St Michael and St George
KOYLI	King's Own Yorkshire Light Infantry
MC	Military Cross
MM	Military Medal
NCO	Non Commissioned Officer

OBE	Officer of the Most Excellent Order … Order of the British Empire
OC	Officer Commanding
OF	Officer Commanding
OR	Other Ranks
PH	Phenate Hexamine helmet (Anti–gas)
PUO	Pyrexia of Uncertain Origin
QM	Quartermaster
RAF	Royal Air Force
RAMC	Royal Army Medical Corps
RE	Royal Engineers
RFC	Royal Flying Corps
RMS	Royal Mail Ship
RQMS	Regimental Quartermaster Sergeant
RSM	Regimental Sergeant Major
SMLE	Short Magazine Lee Enfield
VAD	Voluntary Aid Detachment
YMCA	Young Men's Christian Association

Introduction

Numerous battalion histories were written in the decade following the end of the First World War, very often by ex-members of the battalion. Most of these works used the recollections of former members of the battalion and, of course, the battalion's war diary as the basic framework on which to hang the story of battles fought and hideous conditions endured. Regimental *esprit de corps* often influenced the authors to emphasise those occasions when the battalion performed at its peak, received commendations from commanding generals and individuals were rewarded with medals.

The original author of this book, Captain R. Ede England, was a local man educated at Queen Elizabeth Grammar School in Wakefield (1904–06), as were his two brothers Edward and Benjamin both of whom served in and survived the war. His father, Harry England, originally from Sheffield, was a Tramways Manager who worked for a time in Bolton, Lancashire, where all three brothers were born. Captain England's book entitled, *A Brief History of the 12th Bn, King's Own Yorkshire Light Infantry (Pioneers) "The Miners Battalion"*, was originally printed by John Lindley, Ltd, of Wakefield. The original publication is thought to have been produced sometime during the late 1920s and, at the present time, it is believed that only three copies survive. Most of the photographs in the first edition are copies of originals taken by members of the Battalion and are what the Imperial War Museum describes as 'tipped in', meaning they are not attached securely to the page. Over the intervening years, and particularly during the preparation of this new edition, the King's Own Yorkshire Light Infantry (KOYLI) museum has been given many of the remaining photographs included in the book.

At the time that Captain England was completing his history of the 12th (Service) Battalion King's Own Yorkshire Light Infantry, Siegfried Sassoon's *Memoirs of a Foxhunting Man* was published (1928), followed by

Robert Graves' *Goodbye to All That* (1929). Both authors had served in the same battalion, 2nd Royal Welch Fusiliers, and both criticised the politicians and senior army commanders for the huge loss of life. Recalling Armistice night 1918 Graves wrote, 'The news sent me out walking alone…cursing and sobbing and thinking of the dead.' David Lloyd George, who became the British Prime Minister in December 1916, had numerous disagreements with the Commander-in-Chief (C-in-C) Sir Douglas Haig. Lloyd George considered Haig to be responsible for the huge loss of British lives during the great battles of the Somme, Arras and Third Ypres, and in 1933 he published the first volume of his *War Memoirs*. In chapter XXXVII, 1914–1916: A Retrospect, Lloyd George wrote, 'With a criminal prodigality we had squandered the superior manpower that had been at our disposal.' In early 1917 Lloyd George went so far as to attempt to place the British Army under the command of the French General Nivelle, albeit temporarily, but his scheme failed.

In 1964, to mark the fiftieth anniversary of the outbreak of the First World War, the BBC produced its twenty-six episode television documentary *The Great War*. With a script written by the military historians John Terraine and Correlli Barnett, the programmes not only prompted an interest in the story of the war, it also initiated a growth in the study of the war from the political, economic, military and civilian perspectives. Men of all ranks recounted how they had fought and survived through the terrible conditions that had prevailed. The programme resulted in a revival of interest in all aspects of the war, the increase of academic studies of the whole period and a renewal of the writing of battalion histories – especially those of the 'Pals' battalions.

Captain England's description of the Battalion's wartime experience is somewhat different to that of most authors of such works. Dr William Mitchinson, in his excellent study *Pioneer Battalions in the Great War* (1997), refers to two battalion histories, that of the 17th Battalion Northumberland Fusiliers, and the 12th KOYLI, suggesting that both are 'written in a lighter vein, neither hesitates to poke fun at itself when the situation offered an opportunity'. Captain England's approach to the telling of the story and the horrors of the war does, at times, appear somewhat light-hearted but this may simply reflect his ability to see a lighter side to the grim reality that was all around him. This was not unusual for throughout the war British soldiers were known to have sung humorous and often bawdy songs as they trudged along the roads of northern France. Also, there were many comical articles published in *The Wipers Times,* a newspaper compiled and produced by officers and men of 12th Battalion Sherwood Foresters. This battalion was also a Pioneer battalion and served with the 24th Infantry Division throughout the war. Another source of First World War humour can be seen in the many cartoons created by Bruce Bairnsfather, an officer in the Royal Warwickshire Regiment until he was wounded and evacuated to England after the Second Battle of Ypres in 1915.

In late 1914 and early 1915, the fighting on the Western Front developed into static warfare as both sides constructed deep trenches and dugouts to protect themselves from the artillery barrages of their opponents. Originally raised as an infantry battalion the 12th KOYLI was designated a Pioneer battalion in April 1915, and while the majority of the men appeared to have no objection to this fundamental change from infantry to Pioneers, there were some who were annoyed when they realized that they were not to be allowed to get to close quarters with the enemy as ordinary infantrymen.

During the early years of the war recruits in the newly formed Kitchener infantry battalions were drawn from all walks of life; light and heavy industries, construction, commerce, the retail trade etc, but in none of these industries was the deliberate taking or saving of life, multiple deaths, and fearful mutilations part of their day-to-day experience. Infantry training attempted to overcome some of the particular problems experienced in warfare by teaching men how to work in groups for their own safety, and how to respond when they and their comrades were faced by a determined enemy bent on their destruction. Static warfare required suitable road and rail links between the rear supply depots and the artillery and infantry at the front. As both sides increasingly used heavy artillery to destroy their opponent's defensive trench systems there grew a need for deeper trenches and underground bunkers, and who better to construct these than experienced miners. They were skilled in the use of explosives underground, in the laying of roads and narrow gauge rail tracks, in the laying of water pipes and, should the need arise, they knew how to react when an emergency occurred. Also, in the event of an explosion underground they instinctively knew how to work as a team and were familiar with escaping gas, the rescue of buried workmates and some had basic ambulance training. At the turn of the century the coal industry was beginning to respond more actively to the problem of accidents down the mines. One organisation that made a significant contribution was the West Riding Coal Owners' Association, who were also responsible for raising the Battalion in 1914. In 1911, this Association spent £13,000 on building a new training centre at Altofts Colliery in West Yorkshire to train special Mine Rescue Teams. The day-to-day experiences of these men in their peacetime occupation all too often included some of the traumatic experiences that would become part of every day life in the trenches. It should also be remembered that the mining communities from which these men came were used to dealing with the sudden death of their menfolk, and the response of the families within those communities was traditionally of the highest order. It was these aspects of their background in civilian life that made these men particularly suitable for the job they were asked to perform on the battlefield.

Unlike many of the Kitchener battalions, the 12th KOYLI had excellent facilities for their first experience of army life, all of which were generously provided by their former employers. Captain England explains some little known aspects of life in the British Army during the First World War. In Chapter II he refers to an officer's 'batman', a term more often associated with the Second World War, whereas in World War One the term most often used was 'servant'. The difference in this instance may result from the fact that these men, officers and soldiers alike, were used to working with each other in close proximity down the mines where, in such a hostile environment, they needed to rely on each other, especially in times of crisis when social standing was the least of their problems. Captain England also uses the word 'musketry', and his own invented 'muskatorial', when referring to the many do's and don'ts in the firing of a rifle. The word musketry is still in use by the army, despite the fact that the musket was superseded by the breach-loading rifle many years before the First World War began.

As the war progressed, the magnitude of the problems facing the Pioneers increased. As each warring nation was forced to commit more of its resources to the conflict, so the tasks facing those supporting the frontline troops grew in size and importance. In Chapter XII, Captain England quotes casualty figures sustained by the warring nations. He attributes the huge increase to the use of artillery, especially heavy guns, and the consequent improvements in shell production together with the development of quick firing infantry weapons. In 1914 each battalion of infantry (approximately 850 men) had two machine guns, each served by a section of six men, but the rest of the men were armed with rifles and bayonets. By 1915 the number of machine guns was increased to four, with the number of men needed to operate them increasing accordingly. By 1918, the machine guns had been organised into a Machine Gun Corps and were no longer under the command of ordinary infantry battalions. By 1918, the British infantry battalion had undergone a number of changes with each platoon now having a Lewis gun section, a rifle section, a rifle-grenade section and a bombing section (hand thrown grenades). The actual battlefields of the war covered huge areas in Europe, Russia and the Middle East, and to maintain the vast armies that were raised by all the participating nations, arms and munitions were required on an industrial scale. Consequently, when these weapons were employed on the battlefield the men from all the participating nations were killed on an industrial scale.

Captain England also refers to the extent of the damage to the towns and cities of northern France, and even to the very nature of the soil over which the battles were fought. This reveals his insight into the nature of the conflict that was waged over four years that produced conditions that had never before been experienced. Some idea of industrialized warfare can be gained from Captain England's figures showing that, during the Third Battle of Ypres in 1917, the 12th KOYLI laid 29 miles of light railway track (not including the many repairs needed to keep this track in service throughout the battle) and that on one week alone this particular railway system, only one of many, carried some 18,000 tons of ammunition. Captain England's casualty figures for all the nations involved in the war, quoted in Chapter XII , may have been the best assessment available at the time. However, even after one hundred years of study it is still not possible to give exact figures for any of the participating nations but, considering the data available at the time, Captain England's are somewhere in the region of the accepted figures today.

In Appendix I, 'Functions of a Pioneer Battalion', Captain England outlines the many and varied aspects of the work of Pioneer Battalions during the First World War. He quite forcibly points out that both the men and their officers were more than capable of carrying out the many task the British Army required of them; indeed, they were trained professionals at performing some of these tasks long before the Army realized that such work would become vital if it was to succeed in the industrialized style of warfare that lay ahead of them.

The British Army has a long history of needing the particular skills of the Pioneers. The British Army also has a reputation for expecting too much from too few and in the case of the 12th KOYLI, in the desperate days of the German offensive of April 1918, the men of this battalion were required to fight as infantrymen. On this occasion they were not found wanting. Considering that at one time the battalion numbers grew to 1,300, their total casualties for the whole war were well below those of most infantry battalions. However, the importance of their role within the army as a whole can be seen today for, as General Sir Hugh Beach points out in his Foreword to Dr Mitchinson's book *Pioneer Battalions in the Great War,* after being disbanded after World War One their role had to be re-introduced during the Second World War and today the Royal Logistics Corps (formed in April 1993) supplies all the many support groups that the modern army requires. Indeed, the word logistics is in common usage in many aspects of everyday life in the 21st Century.

The original readers of Captain England's book would have been familiar with the political, social and industrial background of the time. For example, many of the ex-soldiers and their families would have been familiar with such names as 'Maconochie's stew', only one of a number of canned foodstuffs produced by the Maconochie Company but one that developed an unfortunate reputation with the troops. The brand may be unfamiliar to many people in the 21st Century therefore, wherever this or other references require more detailed explanation, I have used square brackets [–] to offer an explanation.

Malcolm K. Johnson

Chapter One

Genesis of the World War – Division of opinion in Britain – War declared on Germany – Mobilization of the Fleet

On 29 June, 1914, the people of the British Isles were shocked by the news of the assassination in Sarajevo (Bosnia) on the previous day of the Arch-Duke Francis Ferdinand of Austria. Comparatively few of them realised that the crime might be the excuse that would lead to a war in Europe, and the weeks which elapsed before Austria made any significant move encouraged the belief that the effects would be isolated and localized. Domestic affairs, notably the apparent threat of civil war in Ireland, and the Dublin affray of 26 July, [when an Irish Nationalist Youth organisation openly displayed 900 Mauser rifles imported from Germany] absorbed the attention of the general public, and not until the very last days of July did the British people awake to the fact that a great European war was impending; even then the general expectation was that Great Britain would not be involved. On 31 July, the Liberal British Prime Minister, Mr H.H. Asquith, announced that the issues of peace and war were hanging in the balance, and that it was of vital importance that the United Kingdom should present a united front. But the implications of the Entente with France were by no means generally understood. Some of our leading newspapers insisted on the necessity of Britain standing by France, while others protested vehemently against any departure from neutrality: the Cabinet was as divided as the public. On Saturday, 1 August, Germany declared war on France. A hurried meeting of the Unionist [Conservative] Opposition dispatched a letter to the Government offering their unhesitating support to any measure necessary for standing by France and Russia. On 3 August, the Foreign Minister (Sir Edward Grey) made his historic speech which finally convinced the country, and indeed all patriots throughout the Empire, of the righteousness of the cause, and Mr Redmond, leader of the Irish Nationalist Party in the House of Commons, made his dramatic announcement that Irish feeling towards England had completely changed, and that the British troops might be safely withdrawn from Ireland. The only objectors to our playing an honourable part in the distasteful business into which we had very reluctantly been drawn were sundry Liberals, and some few members of the Socialist Party, headed by Mr Ramsey Macdonald.

On 4 August, Great Britain issued her ultimatum to Germany to respect Belgian neutrality, and when Germany refused, she declared war amid unprecedented excitement throughout the country. The Navy was already mobilized, thanks to the foresight of the First Lord of the Admiralty (Mr Winston Churchill) and the First Sea Lord (Prince Louis of Battenberg) who had delayed its dispersal after a colossal review by H.M. King George V at Spithead. The ships proceeded at once to their stations in the North Sea and the English Channel, and a blockade of Germany was set up. The manner in which our Navy did its hazardous work during the following four years is a matter of history, and forms a glorious chapter in the history of our country.

Chapter 2

Birth of the New Armies – Lord Kitchener's Shrewd Judgement – Shortage of Stores and Equipment – Beginnings of the 12th Battalion King's Own Yorkshire Light Infantry – Lieutenant Colonel R.C. Dill – Early training Burton Leonard – Move to Salisbury Plain – Orders to proceed overseas

The British Army was decidedly small, when compared with those of the major nations of Europe, and quite inadequate for its immediate role in a great continental war. The British Expeditionary Force (BEF), about 150,000 strong, commanded by Sir John French, was, however, quite ready. In response to public demand, Lord Kitchener, [proconsul of Egypt] who was on the point of returning to Egypt after a visit to London, was appointed Secretary of State for War. Without more ado this wonderful man rendered to his country, and to the world, two inestimable services; first, by overcoming both Press and Cabinet opposition to sending English troops to fight in France, and dispatching the Expeditionary Force in perfect security and safety by 21 August. Secondly, by bidding the British Empire to prepare for three years of war, and raise troops to be reckoned in millions rather than thousands. He commenced the formation and organisation of a New Army (popularly known as 'Kitchener's Army') and, due very largely to his personal hold upon the imaginations of the people, recruiting was general and extraordinarily brisk throughout the remainder of the year. [At the time of writing, Captain England may not have known that the decision to send British troops to fight alongside the French in the event of war with Germany, and their safe arrival in France, was in large part the result of secret Anglo–French staff talks which began as early as 1906, long before Kitchener arrived at the War Office.] The sudden demand upon existing stores of military equipment could not be met, and large bodies of enlisted men did all their preliminary training without rifles, uniforms or equipment.

In addition to private individuals, associations of every description rose to the occasion. One such was the West Yorkshire Coal Owners' Association, a body representative of practically all the colliery proprietors in the West Riding of Yorkshire. [At this time the West Riding contained the whole of the present West Yorkshire, South Yorkshire and parts of East and North Yorkshire.] Under the leadership and inspiring example of their Chairman, Mr. C.B. Crawshaw of Dewsbury, this patriotic assembly of business men very quickly came to the conclusion that they could best help in that time of trouble by raising and equipping a complete battalion of infantry. This task they put in hand without delay, and thus was born the 12th (Service) Battalion King's Own Yorkshire Light Infantry.

A small committee was formed to deal with the project, and they for the most part did the work of raising and equipping the embryo unit. This was no child's play by any means, as will be realised when it is stated that the Association actually provided everything for the Battalion eg. the hutments, clothing, military equipment, food and even pay, and this went on until the Battalion was taken over officially by the War Office [12 September 1914]. The Association was informed by Earl Kitchener that it would also be required to find all the officers for the new Battalion, including the Commanding Officer himself, subject to the approval of the War Office. Such was the task which the West Yorkshire Coal Owners shouldered voluntarily, and we must agree that they carried it through magnificently.

In spite of the terrific difficulties encountered on every hand, in spite of the tremendous drain on the country's stocks of leather and cloth, a demand which caused many units to be without uniform of any kind for months, the Association managed to find a firm able to manufacture the web equipment after having, as Captain J.C. Crawshaw said, 'hunted the country over'. The generosity of the Association did not stop here; within a few weeks of arriving at Farnley they provided us with up-to-date signalling apparatus and other things which less fortunate units had to go without. The total net expenditure was somewhere about £10,000.

The first essential was the appointment of a Commanding Officer; the War Office authorities entrusted this to the Coal Owners, whose choice fell upon Lieutenant Colonel R.C. Dill, a distinguished officer of wide experience in many parts of the globe. Headquarters were temporarily established at the

offices of Messrs. Ben Day & Co. in Central Bank Chambers, Leeds. From
here Lieutenant Colonel Dill directed the preliminary spade-work and one
of his first acts was to appoint Captain A. Lyon Campbell as Adjutant, and
Lieutenant A. Ripley as Quartermaster.

There was no camp available for the men, so they were formally enlisted
and then sent back to their civilian occupations until such time as a camp
was ready. Whilst so enlisted they received an allowance of a guinea [£1.05p]
a week. Certain gentlemen, who afterwards became officers of the Battalion,
did splendid recruiting work in their respective areas, notably Mr J.C.
Crawshaw around Dewsbury and Mr D.T.H. Prothero, who recruited no
less than 300 men in the Featherstone district. The majority of the men were
colliers, hard sons of toil and richly endowed with all the sterling qualities of

A working party in overalls, Farnley Camp, 1915. Second row left (seated) with pipe is
Private George Barber Wood. It is obvious that most of these men are in the 25–35 age group
and would be experienced miners or engineers.

the true Englishman. The war caused many changes and provided numerous surprises, but none so great to us as the discovery in these men of a wonderful spirit, a great readiness to learn, an ability to endure great hardships with true cheerfulness and, in the main, a really remarkable adaptability to military discipline. When one considers the general circumstances under which the collier lives and works, it is truly inspiring to think of the magnificent loyalty and obedience shown by these fine men towards the strange, and mostly inexperienced, young officers under whom they found themselves. Many of our men were by no means young, more than a few had reached their half-century in life and had only succeeded in passing the attestation officer by falsifying their true age; many had seen service in other of Britain's big and little wars, but each and all were obviously out to do what they could, and to do it well.

Naturally, amongst so many men embarked upon a new life, there occurred various amusing episodes, but we hope that there was no doubting the facts in the story of the day when a man presented himself to the Quartermaster's stores. 'Well, what the h—— do you want?' inquired the sergeant pleasantly. 'Please, sir', blurted out the rookie, 'I've come to be measured for my sentry box.' Sad to relate, history records no information as to what became of this poor private, but we fancy he was never seen alive again.

Whilst the men and officers were being gathered together, the Coal Owners had secured a site for the camp in the beautiful park surrounding Farnley Hall, near Otley (Yorks.), the ancestral home of Major H.F. Fawkes. J.P. Wooden huts were speedily erected on ground sloping gently towards the River Wharfe, and on 3 November 1914, the first party of men marched in. On this date also, the Battalion was officially mobilized, and on 5 November its name was changed from 12th Miners Battalion, KOYLI, to 12th (Service) Battalion (Miners) (Pioneers), KOYLI. A list of the officers, together with their respective companies, is given below.

Lieutenant Colonel R.C. Dill, Commanding Officer.
Major T. W. Simpson, Second in Command.
Captain. A. Lyon Campbell, Adjutant.
Lieutenant A. Riplev, Quartermaster.
Lieutenant E. Forbes, R.A.M.C., Medical Officer.

A COMPANY.
Major J.S. Charlesworth OC
Lieutenant. J.C. Crawshaw
Second Lieutenant J.A. Hudson
Second Lieutenant G.S. Leach
Second Lieutenant J.S. L. Welsh
Second Lieutenant F. H. White

B COMPANY.
Captain D.T.H. Prothero OC
Second Lieutenant G.T. Simmonds
Second Lieutenant D.E. Roberts
Second Lieutenant A.W. Armitage
Second Lieutenant H.D. Gaunt
Second Lieutenant W. Cooper

C COMPANY.
Captain C.B. Charlesworth OC
Second Lieutenant S.Q. Newton.
Second Lieutenant P.C. Binns
Second Lieutenant J.H. Frank.
Second Lieutenant A. Carnelly
Second Lieutenant A.H. Thompson

D COMPANY.
Captain H.F. Chadwick OC
Second Lieutenant H.R. Burrill
Second Lieutenant B. Mason.
Second Lieutenant R.E. England
Second Lieutenant Q. A. Wright
Second Lieutenant J.W. Talbot

The men were accommodated in forty wooden huts, each about sixty feet long by twenty feet wide and heated by a stove. Each hut housed thirty men and was in reality a barrack room, for in the early days the men had their meals in them. They were raised from the ground on concrete piles, had a double thickness in walls and floors, and with the exterior covered with stout felting they were absolutely weatherproof. The officers' quarters were similar in construction and appearance, except that the sleeping quarters were divided into cubicles, each taking two officers. Their batmen were lodged in a large room at one end of the hut. Other buildings in the camp included a cookhouse fitted with the best-known pattern of cooking range and boiler for 1,000 men, a library, recreation room, gymnasium, store rooms, canteens, regimental offices and guard rooms, and a well-appointed rifle range. The whole camp was lighted with electricity transmitted through overhead wires, and water was laid on from the Farnley Hall mains. For training purposes the camp was most excellently situated, for we had on the one side arable land and undulating pasture, and on the other the hilly country and the moors of Otley Chevin [a steep ridge on the south side of Wharfedale in West Yorkshire] and adjacent ridges. Another advantage

A group of officers at Farnley Camp – 1915. Third from the right, centre row, is believed to be Major T.W. Simpson; on his right is Lieutenant Colonel R.C. Dill, and on his right is believed to be Major J.S. Charlesworth.

The officers of 12th KOYLI at Farnley Camp, 1915. Most of the officers have already grown moustaches and many of the remainder would obey the Army Council Instructions to 'keep the upper lip unshaven'.

Recruits, wearing a mixture of military (blue) and civilian dress, displaying their skill with pick and shovel at Farnley Camp.

was the absence of any very large town close at hand, so that the counter-attractions to military discipline were not too powerful.

During November and December drafts of men marched into camp daily and were received by Lieutenant Colonel Dill, who addressed each batch with soldierly words of advice and encouragement. A certain number of the enlisted men were ex-soldiers; some had held non-commissioned rank, and these were quickly given promotion to enable them to act as instructors. Training could now begin in real earnest, and with infantry exercises and field days time passed pleasantly enough and quickly, and remarkably good progress was made. We all were, of course, extremely impatient to be off to the front, but when in due course we did get there, and had been in close touch with war for barely a week, some of us began to think that this impatience had been rather a mistake!

Seven young officers at Farnley Camp, two are wearing their regulation 1897 pattern infantry officer's sword. The officer smoking, and without his swagger stick and hat, is Second Lieutenant D.E. Roberts.

Almost the first thing we had to learn was how to stand to attention, a much harder accomplishment than one might think. The position of the hands was of immense importance. A little book called Infantry Training contained the most minute directions on the subject, although one sergeant-major was a little off the track when he was heard to reprove a meek and mild private in the following manner: 'Put yer 'ands be'ind the seams of yer trousers, No. 6! What the 'ell do you think the seams of yer trousers are put there for?'

One of our sham fights in particular sticks in the memory. The scene of the action was the Park and its immediate vicinity, which was held by A and D Companies, whose dispositions, it appeared afterwards, were somewhat erratic. B Company, under Captain Prothero, was to force a way through the

Part of a company wearing their original blue uniforms. Standing at ease is Private William Davis (front row, second right).

armed cordon and earlier that evening had marched out of camp. It was a dark and miserable night, and the slightly nervous defending troops waited patiently for a sign of the enemy. Not a sound was heard save the moaning of the wind in the trees. Suddenly, an unearthly yell was succeeded by a terrific fusillade of blanks being fired, and followed by a wild chorus of victory. The defenders, however, remained quite unmoved and unshaken, for it became clear that the attackers had captured a sewage farm that was quite unoccupied by any garrison and, moreover, was on the wrong side of the river! Subsequently, the exhausted victors waded through the chilly waters at a most unexpected place and were discovered drying by the fire when the defenders returned to camp.

Camp life was an entirely novel experience for most of us, but it was remarkable with what speed and enthusiasm both officers and men adapted to the military style of life. We were all acutely aware of the great help given to all by our Commanding Officer (CO), and by Captain Lyon Campbell, the

A Company 12th KOYLI under Sergeant Hughes at Farnley Camp.

Adjutant. Without any special effort we seemed to learn almost immediately the various bugle calls; some such as 'Come to the cook-house door boys', and 'There's no parade today', were perhaps received more kindly than others, for example, 'Reveille', 'Officers come and be damned', or even 'Fall in'.

Lieutenants Burrill and Cooper were detailed to attend a musketry course at Strensall Barracks, near York. The course lasted for three weeks, after which they returned absolutely bursting with knowledge musketorial [rifle drill] which they passed on to a class of officers who were then turned loose upon their respective companies. It was no easy matter to instruct stolid Yorkshire miners in the art of – *the lying load, the kneeling load, the six o'clock aim*, or the mysteries of the *triangle of error*. [The British Army's Musketry Regulations required an infantryman to be able to fire fifteen rounds at a target four feet square within one minute; the number of hits determined whether they were graded First or Second Class marksmen. This exercise was sometimes referred to as 'The Mad Minute'. The record for 1909 was thirty-six hits in one minute. It was this level of skill that surprised the Germans during their initial engagements with the British Expeditionary Force at Mons and Le Cateau in 1914.] About February [1915], the first modern rifle, the Short Magazine Lee Enfield (SMLE) arrived in the camp. This rare specimen was carefully placed in the custody of the Adjutant, and officers requiring the use of this weapon for lectures or fondling purposes, were required to sign a book at the Orderly Room.

There is only one parade in the Army to which men rush to be present; that is Sick Parade. Every morning early the Doctor held a kind of levée and we very quickly formed the conclusion that a certain pill known as a No. 9 was truly the most remarkable curative agent known to medicine, since it was prescribed in single or double numbers for anything from an in-growing toe nail to appendicitis. The Army had other pills for other ailments not included in this range, and it is said that on the occasions when the Doctor had temporarily exhausted his stock of No. 9s the deficiency was made good by the issue of a No. 4 and a No. 5!

The Coal Owners' Association very generously provided a Wolseley touring car for the use of the officers, and right good use they made of it for visiting Leeds and Harrogate. It has been suggested that, with Lieutenant.

All Pioneers had to learn to shoot straight and the 'Triangle of Errors' apparatus shown here helped them so to do.

P.C. Binns seated next to the driver, the car was a familiar and welcome sight to members of the local police force as it made its nocturnal journeys to and from these towns. One of the most popular of Army customs is – leave of absence, and some of our men discovered remarkably ingenious reasons why they should be allowed a week-end at home. We have heard of the office boy who always contrived to bury an aunt whenever the local football team had a big match on, but everything pales into insignificance besides the example of the man who went before Lieutenant Colonel Dill with an important telegram, 'Come at once – father dead'. After being granted four days leave, and being on the point of marching out, the Colonel asked the man how long his father had been dead. To which the enterprising mourner replied, after much hesitation: 'Seven years!'

In the middle of January 1915, real khaki service dress and rifles were issued to the men, who up to this time had been clothed in a blue serge uniform of a peculiar design and only the officers wore khaki outfits. With the arrival of our actual uniforms and rifles we were at last able to regard ourselves with pardonable pride as fully-fledged soldiers. Meanwhile, the troops at the front were in desperate need of men skilled in the art of digging and other tasks of a semi-technical nature. Our men were naturally past masters at digging, and therefore, in April 1915, the unit was created a Pioneer Battalion, and several officers with practical civil engineering experience were obtained by Lieutenant Colonel Dill. Henceforward, the nature of our daily exercises took on a somewhat different aspect, and we received detailed instruction in elementary field engineering. Perhaps it will be as well if we here describe what a Pioneer Battalion really was.

The Pioneer Infantry Battalion, an organisation closely associated with the Royal Engineers (RE), though never actually incorporated therein, was intended to be supplementary to RE labour, and to be normally associated much more closely than other infantry with the Field Companies, Royal Engineers. This was based on the practice, well known in India, where such battalions trained to a much greater extent in field engineering than the average line battalions. [This innovation was introduced by Lord Kitchener when he was Commander-in-Chief of the Indian Army, 1902–1909, and had proved to be most useful.] Broadly speaking, the duties of the pioneer battalion were the construction of field defences of every type and in every part of the forward zone; the making of temporary roads, bridges and railways, and the carrying out of demolitions. It was never intended that the pioneer troops should be used as infantry except in the gravest emergency, but in many instances this was not borne in mind, and the resulting casualties made the lack of such technical troops more acutely felt than ever. There was one pioneer battalion to each division; a divisional commander had thus at his disposal a sufficient supply of skilled labour for him to make tactical use of engineering works. Major-General Sir George K. Scott-Moncrieff, KCB, KCMG, CIE, had written, 'As regards the officers, the greater their knowledge and experience in engineering work the better, owing to the variety of work that fell upon their shoulders. The development of weapons and the weight of guns which came to be used in the war revolutionised much of the previous practice; no longer were combinations of timber, brushwood and earth sufficient for field defences, nor pontoons and spar bridges sufficient to cross rivers. Concrete and steel had come into the field, and engineers accustomed to using them in peace time had to take them in hand for war, and to see that rapidity of construction was combined with stability and strength.'

In May 1915, Lieutenant Colonel Dill was advised on medical grounds to resign the command of the Battalion. No words of ours can describe the affection in which we held our Commanding Officer; there was not a single young officer in the unit who could not recall some occasion on which our dearly-beloved Commander had, by his great tact and almost fatherly advice, set his feet upon the right path. Remarkable was the esteem in which he was held by the non-commissioned officers and men, who had learnt, by reason of his firmness no less than by his justness, his deep understanding of their trials and tribulations, not merely to obey him as their commanding officer, but to know him as a friend. During his association with us were sown the seeds of that great loyalty and discipline which were destined to bear such magnificent fruit later on in the test of war.

Just before he left, Lieutenant Colonel Dill, on behalf of the officers, and as a mark of appreciation of the many kindnesses extended to the Battalion by the citizens of Otley, entertained a number of representative townsmen to dinner. The inhabitants of the town had been extraordinarily good to us all, and we felt very grateful to them. A week or so before we left Farnley

Park a fifth Company, known as E (Reserve) Company, was formed under the command of Captain Lampen. It had to be officered, and those who were chosen accepted their lot with no great enthusiasm, since it was almost certain that they would not proceed overseas with the rest of the Battalion. This Company eventually grew into a battalion, thanks to an intensive recruiting campaign, and we believe that more than a little credit for the success achieved was due to Lieutenant J.A. Hudson, who alone swore in 980 men. Amongst the officers who were chosen to serve with E Company were Second Lieutenants A.H. Thompson and A.W. Armitage, both were killed at the Battle of the Somme. [Captain A.H. Thompson served with 9th KOYLI, Second Lieutenant A.W. Armitage with 2nd KOYLI]

Lieutenant Colonel G.E.L. Gilbert, who succeeded Lieutenant Colonel Dill.

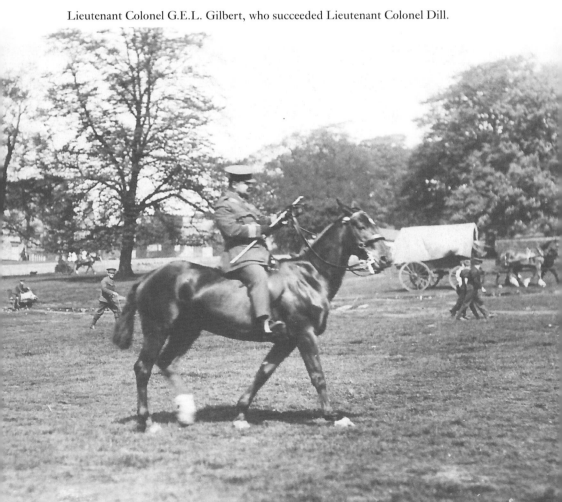

Lieutenant Colonel R.C. Dill was succeeded by Lieutenant Colonel G.E.L. Gilbert DSO, of the Indian Army, and almost immediately upon taking up his duties we moved by route march to a canvas camp at Burton Leonard, three miles south of Ripon (Yorks.). Here we began to construct a series of five rifle ranges, on which many thousands of British lads first learnt the use of that weapon with which they afterwards acquitted themselves so splendidly on many battlefields throughout the world. The men did not take too kindly to this digging work, as their main desire was to get to France before the war was over. As they said, 'They had joined the army to fight, not to dig.' They used to sing a little ditty, which went like this:

Lieutenant Colonel Gilbert with the officers of 12th KOYLI. Seated front row second from the right is Lieutenant D.E. Roberts and his brother, Second Lieutenant William H. Roberts, is back row second from the right.

At least two companies stand at ease while their senior officers, mounted, have a discussion. Farnley Camp 1915.

> Kitchener's army – shillin' a day,
> Up at reveille, workin' all t'day,
> An' if us grumbles what do they say?
> Shove 'im int' guard-room – stop 'im 'is pay.

Soon after Colonel Gilbert arrived he disbanded the bugle band and instructed Major J.S. Charlesworth to form a brass band. [This was contrary to the custom of most Light Infantry Regiments which usually include a bugle in their regimental badge, and had used bugles since the Napoleonic War, preferring them to drums for transmitting commands on the battlefield.] Musical talent sprang from the ranks in plenty, and we quickly had a combination which could produce recognisable music. The band gave its first public display on a certain guest night when Admiral Sir Francis B. Bridgeman, GCB, GCVO, who resided at Copgrove Hall close by, was the guest of honour. An ambitious programme was attempted and, although discord was sometimes apparent to even the most uncultured ear, their efforts were greatly appreciated. Our church parades were a feature of the times and were held in a huge marquee. Once the service was over, the whole Battalion, headed by the band, which had really become remarkably proficient, marched around the camp watched by an admiring crowd of civilians. The camp at Burton Leonard was very pleasantly situated in a large field of pasture, although perhaps not near enough to a town as some of the younger men in the Battalion would have wished. Our task, the construction of the five rifle ranges, was one of some magnitude and it was necessary to work through the night; this we did by the light of numerous large acetylene burners, which had a nasty habit of bubbling over in an alarming manner and then going off 'pop'. Combined with the constructional work were infantry exercises to keep us in touch with the military side of life and to maintain discipline – the great characteristic which distinguishes an army from a rabble. Many times afterwards the unit was complimented by general officers on its splendid discipline.

[In 1901, the country was divided into six regional commands with Northern Command Headquarters being in York. Lord Kitchener's First New Army (known as K1) included the 11th (Northern) Division, which

The Burton Leonard Camp, Ripon showing the 600 yards firing point, 1915.

was formed by Northern Command and joined K1. The 17th (Northern) Division was also formed by Northern Command and became part of K2.] The Northern Command was constantly requiring returns and on one occasion a list of married and single men was asked for. A Company was paraded and lined up two deep. 'On the command "March" single men step one pace forward, married men step one pace back', said the Sergeant Major. The order was given and the Company moved with the exception of one man who remained perfectly still. 'Now then, Private O'Brien', yelled the Sergeant Major, 'why the blazes don't you move – didn't you hear the order?' 'S'hure', says Paddy, 'I'm neither'. 'What the devil are you then?' says the Sergeant Major. 'I'm livin' tally,' says Paddy.

In August, on a day which will never be forgotten by those who participated, we were inspected in musketry by a staff officer from York,

A group of officers relax outside their tent at Burton Leonard. Lieutenant D.E. Roberts, again without his hat and smoking his pipe, is fourth from the left.

who expressed himself as much impressed by what he saw! [Muskets were last used in the British Army in the 1860s, but the term musketry continued to be used in certain circumstances up to the end of the twentieth century and beyond. This was particularly so in the Light Infantry regiments who prided themselves in the speed and accuracy of their rifle fire.] While at Farnley Park the catering for the officers' mess had been done by a firm of contractors, but on our removal to Burton Leonard this convenience ceased and a Mess President, assisted by a small committee, took over the duties. They commenced under difficulties, for they were unused to the job and, moreover, the food had to be prepared in field ovens and served in a marquee. We could, therefore, hardly expect the cooking to be of such a high order as that at Farnley but our Mess President did very well indeed and we all tried to persuade ourselves that the food was quite as fine if not better than we had been used to. The Medical Officer at that time, Lieutenant F.W. Wesley, would always express the opinion that each dish placed before him, no matter how strange, was the finest he had ever tasted. Complete disaster nearly befell the Mess one day when an elephant belonging to a travelling circus came past the camp. The mess tent was alongside a hedge by the roadside and, smelling the good fare provided for us, Jumbo did some good scouting with his trunk and had put away three days' rations in five minutes before the mess cook rushed out and landed him one with a frying pan.

One fine day we were informed that our transport mules had arrived at Ripon. Lieutenant J.A. Hudson was instructed to take twenty men and bring the animals back to camp. Lieutenant Hudson later gave a humorous account of this experience.

To my consternation I found the mules, some forty in number, packed tight in the trucks, head to tail alternately. How to get these mules the four miles back to camp was a puzzle, as no halters were with the animals. On the advice of Sergeant Charlesworth, I sent down to Ripon and procured stout lengths of cord and tied their necks and tails together in fours, and in such a manner rode the animals through the city of Ripon to the great amusement of the citizens. Our arrival at Burton Leonard was a signal for great excitement. Some of the men forgot their military discipline and evidently thought that the mules had been

A group of volunteers in the khaki uniforms rest outside their tent at the Burton Leonard Camp.

Outside washing arrangements at the Burton Leonard camp.

provided for their personal amusement and various impromptu races were commenced before order and discipline were restored.

From time to time, and at irregular intervals, Army orders were issued by the General Staff. [Captain England was mistaken in this instance. From 1904 onwards an Army Council had been created, in much the same form as the Board of Admiralty, and was chaired by the Secretary of State for War: the Imperial General Staff was also created and it was the Army Council that became the main administrators of the Army and issued this particular order.] Their recommendations occasionally proved trying, particularly when it was ordered that 'officers and men must keep the upper lip unshaven', implying that moustaches were to be worn. The efforts of some very young officers to induce a hearty growth were extremely praiseworthy, though barren of results. The sartorial lapses of Britain's youth were pointed out in an Army Order which consigned 'gor blimey' caps to the dust bin and looked with disfavour on collars, ties and socks not of an approved shade. We fancy that the Adjutant grew thin from trying to enforce these decrees, for which we must admit there was much justification. We might explain that a 'gor blimey' is a type of headgear which, when on the head, looks like a dirty pudding cloth with a piece of cardboard stuck on one side. It is related that one officer, having acquired a nice new shiny motor-cycle, and anxious to make a smart turn-out, went off to the nearest Ordnance Depot. There he examined caps, hundreds of them, explaining as he departed that what he wanted was 'one with a peak at the back'. [In the winter of 1915, the Army issued a cap with large flaps on either side which could be tied under the chin to provide extra warmth. On reaching France, many young officers took the wire stiffener out of their peaked caps to try to disguise the fact that they were inexperienced newcomers to the frontline.]

In September of 1915, Lieutenant Colonel Gilbert was transferred to 11th Entrenching Battalion, and Lieutenant Colonel E.L. Chambers, a well-known athlete, was appointed in his place. In due course the ranges were completed, and the Battalion, having attained a high pitch of excellence in drill and battle exercises, was detailed as the Pioneer Battalion of the newly formed 31st Division, then being concentrated at Fovant on Salisbury Plain, whence we were transported by rail on 22 October. Our new camp was noteworthy for the richness and adhesive qualities of the mud; here we carried out final training and musketry practice. Amongst the entertaining diversions was the officer's revolver practice, when they could be seen vainly endeavouring to hit a four-foot target at a range of ten yards.

At the end of November rumours were afloat that we were destined for France, and excitement ran high. It appears to be a fact that part of the Divisional Headquarters had actually gone there, but early in December definite orders were received to proceed overseas at an early date. Much mystery attached to these instructions and our rumoured destinations ranged

Lieutenant Colonel E.L. Chambers, Commanding Officer 12th KOYLI from September 1915–11 August 1917.

from Woolamaloo to the Rocky Mountains. The mystery only thickened on the arrival of a consignment of pith helmets. India was the unanimously agreed destination, and every old soldier we had at once blossomed out a fluent speaker of Hindustani, Sanskrit, Urdu, or any other Indian tongue one liked to mention. We had a suspicion that their vocabularies consisted almost entirely of swear words, and this suspicion was confirmed when we did eventually arrive in the East.

Now there was a great demand upon the services of old Indian campaigners, for did not they know the innermost secrets of the pugaree? This anglicised form of the Hindu 'pagri' denotes a long, long scarf of white or khaki cotton or silk wound round and round a hat or helmet as a protection against the sun. There were apparently great niceties to be observed in the fixation upon the helmet of this accessory, and fierce was the competition to secure the services of the expert fixer of pugarees. This honour fell, we think, to Sergeant Major Madden, of D Company, who long basked contentedly in the sunlight of fame.

During 2, 3 and 4 December, preparations for embarkation proceeded apace. On 5 December Lieutenant Colonel Chambers, with nineteen officers and 599 other ranks (OR), left Dinton Station for Liverpool, where they embarked on HMT *Empress of Britain*, sailing at 10 am on 7 December. The remainder of the Battalion, consisting of ten officers and 408 ORs, proceeded to Devonport and embarked, some on HMT *Minnewaska*, some onboard the *Shropshire*, and others on the *Nessian*; the transport travelled on the *Nessian*. The embarkation strength was thus thirty officers and 1,007 ORs. Below is given a list of the officers who proceeded to Egypt:

Lieutenant Colonel E.L. Chambers, Commanding Officer
Major J.S. Charlesworth, Second in Command
Major C.B. Charlesworth
Captain H.F. Chadwick
Captain G.S. Leach
Captain J.C. Crawshaw
Captain W. Cooper
Captain J.H. Frank
Captain D.E. Roberts
Captain G.M. Stockings
Lieutenant J.S.L. Welch
Lieutenant W.S. Vincent
Lieutenant W.H. Roberts
Lieutenant J. Gaunt
Lieutenant P.T. Crowther
Lieutenant F.H. White
Lieutenant H.D. Gaunt
Lieutenant P.C. Binns
Lieutenant B.Mason
Lieutenant R.E. England
Second Lieutenant L. Forsdike
Second Lieutenant W.E. Oliver
Second Lieutenant J.K. Partridge
Second Lieutenant J.J. McGroarty

Second Lieutenant G. Walker
Second Lieutenant N.L. Bennett
Second Lieutenant V. Mossop
Adjutant: Captain S.Q. Newton
Quartermaster: Lieutenant W. Parkin
Medical Officer: Lieutenant E. Forbes RAMC

Chapter 3

An eventful voyage – Malta. Arrival at Port Said – Camp at Port Said – Those Christmas turkeys – El Kantara – Removal to Hill 70 – Rescue of an aeroplane – Awful sand storms – Defence systems of the Suez Canal – Orders arrive to proceed to France – Voyage to Marseilles

The ships were well-appointed and, speaking broadly, both officers and men were decidedly comfortable, though it must be said that the men on the *Empress of Britain* were not too well off, and did not stand very much chance of escape if the ship had been torpedoed as they were four or five decks down and had about 4,000 troops above them. [The *Empress of Britain* began life as a Royal Mail Ship (RMS) on the transatlantic route. On the outbreak of war she was converted into an armed merchantman and then a troop transporter.] Ocean trips at that time of the year are naturally expected to be a little rough, and it must be admitted that it lived up to our expectations and for the first two days the stewards had the dining saloon almost entirely to themselves.

The submarine menace was a problem, and various methods were employed to locate and destroy any attacker. The *Minnewaska* had two field guns lashed to the fo'c'sle rails; armed military sentries were posted at intervals round the saloon deck and ordered to keep a look-out for any signs of a periscope or torpedo track. A five inch naval gun was mounted on the poop deck and manned by a naval crew. The field guns came into action once only; the officer in charge said that it was positively indecent to carry so much ammunition about and not use it, so we used some, but the shells seemed to almost drop out of the muzzle so vast is the field of vision across the water. The riflemen expended many bullets upon floating bottles, relics of the night before from some unknown ship; and the naval gun was fired

HMT *Minniewaska* was armed with a five inch naval gun mounted on the poop deck.

only once, when it frightened everybody to death. As a matter of precaution all ranks were ordered to sleep wearing their lifebelts, but we had a feeling that the man has yet to be born who can so much as lie down in a lifebelt without suffering all the pains of hell, so we dispensed with this luxurious safety measure, and not a soul wore a belt except when the Captain was looking. At sea we had nothing particular to do except make out returns and count the needles in the men's 'hussifs'. [hussif = the soldier's term for his Housewife (sewing kit) – a small white cotton pack containing needles and thread used for repairs to his kit. It often contained his brass button stick for use when polishing the brass buttons on his tunic.] There was little sniping on the seas, and no land to be seen, so we were pretty thankful when Gibraltar was reached.

By order of the naval authorities boats were permitted to pass through the Straits of Gibraltar after dark only. It is a weird but an interesting experience to be gliding slowly through the water with hardly an exterior sound when suddenly a shaft of intense white light pierces the gloom, ranges rapidly over the ship from stem to stern and then fixes itself upon the bows, where the name of the ship is painted; meanwhile, a stentorian voice enquires testily what ship we are, who the master, of what nationality, and lots of other questions. The source of all the trouble presently looms up alongside and is seen to be a fussy little destroyer, which very quickly completes her business and after a further exchange of light banter with our Captain swirls away into the darkness, leaving us to pursue our course. And what a course too! Once through the Straits we had entered the hot bed of submarine activity, and to baffle any enemy submarine attempting to fire a torpedo our ships altered their courses producing a continuous series of long and short zig-zags. It was this procedure which lengthened the time of our voyage so considerably, but it was necessary and gave one a certain sense of security. At this time there were twelve German submarines operating in the Mediterranean Sea, among them Max Valentier (*U38*) and Arnauld de la Periere, (*U35*), two of the most distinguished enemy submarine commanders. On 18 December, the *Empress of Britain* did actually sight an enemy submarine and fired two shells in her direction, which caused the enemy craft to dive instantly. Few on board knew that at the same time a torpedo fired from a submarine on the other side of the ship missed us by a mere one hundred yards. For the remainder of the voyage our peace of mind was undisturbed by any more such happenings, though these same submarines sank the food ships following us, an act which kept us on short rations for a few weeks.

Four days out from Gibraltar the *Empress* was again in the wars – this time a more serious matter. In the early hours of the morning and with a terrific crash she struck amidships the French schooner *Juperat*. The collision

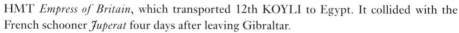

HMT *Empress of Britain*, which transported 12th KOYLI to Egypt. It collided with the French schooner *Juperat* four days after leaving Gibraltar.

brought everybody tumbling out of bed; for all they knew the ship had been torpedoed, indeed, that was the prevailing impression as the shock of the impact lifted her out of the water and caused her to shudder like a living thing. Now was seen the splendid discipline of our men. There was not a trace of panic, and under the circumstances a certain amount would have been understandable. It must be borne in mind that, just before retiring to bed we received the comforting intelligence that we were about to pass through the narrowest and the most dangerous portion of the whole Mediterranean Sea, and the *Empress* with 5,000 troops on board was a prize that submarine commanders would have liked very much to secure.

After eight days steaming from England, Malta was reached on 14 December 1915, and each ship remained in the wonderful Grand Harbour of Valletta for three days. Shore leave was granted and utilised to the full. This three day holiday was the one good thing that came of the *Empress'* misfortunes, as it was necessary to repair the bows of the ship, which had been stove in somewhat. The island of Malta is 7½ miles long by 8½ wide and, seen from the sea in the bright sunlight of early morning, the collection of bright coloured buildings perched on a huge heap of yellow rock and encompassed by the wonderful blue waters of the Mediterranean, made up a beautiful picture. Hardly had our good ships let go the anchors when we were besieged by native merchants of all kinds selling everything from carpets to parrots. The prices demanded were terrific, but they were halved at the slightest sign of wavering on the buyer's part, and still further reduced by a little judicious haggling until, finally, the deal was concluded at a figure which was a mere fraction of the original. Boat loads of small boys in birthday dress cruised round the vessel waiting for someone to throw overboard a handful of silver coins (copper they refused to touch), which they deftly retrieved under water in their toes or in their mouths. So clear was the water that the harbour bottom, fifty feet below the surface, could be plainly seen.

The Maltese are a handsome, well-formed race, about middle height and well set up, the women being generally smaller than the men, with fine black eyes, fine hair and graceful carriage, and all are strict adherents to the Roman Catholic religion. Everyone, both high and low, speaks the native language, Phoenician Maltese. We saw most of the sights, the most impressive being perhaps the old palace of the Grand Masters of the Order of St. John of

Most of the battalion's stores and equipment would be unloaded at El Kantara using this method.

Jerusalem (ie. Knights of Malta), now a museum, and the unique Cathedral of St. John, containing tombs of some of the knights, some very magnificent tapestries, and a quantity of wonderful work in lapis lazuli. [Captain England may not have known that the correct ecclesiastical title is, the Co-Cathedral. Sometime after 1820 the cathedral became a Co-Cathedral, equal in prominence with the archbishop's cathedral at Mdina.] We left the island on 17 December, steamed into Alexandria on 19 December, arrived at Port Said on 21 December 1915 and disembarked the following day.

There were many amongst us whose hearts were too full for words at finding the good dry land beneath our feet once more. Perhaps the thought in everyone's head was, 'Well, here we are in the land of the Pharaohs: it doesn't look very romantic – in fact it looks decidedly dirty.' And dirty it was, as we were soon to discover. Whilst waiting to disembark we witnessed a most extraordinary spectacle in the form of a ship being coaled by natives. There were a couple of coal lighters moored alongside the vessel and planks laid as gangways from one to the other. Up and down these planks was a constant procession of natives in various stages of undress, carrying on their shoulders large baskets of coal. It was wonderful to think that by this primitive method the ship could receive her one hundred tons of fuel, but what was even more remarkable was the extraordinary din which the porters made. They were all singing or howling. Imagine a Hallelujah Chorus of two or three hundred voices, each individual singing a different song and all in different keys, and you have some slight idea of the noise we heard.

Apparently, the reason for our visit to Egypt was this. The evacuation of the Gallipoli peninsula having been ordered on 8 December 1915, it was decided to send the British troops who had been fighting there to Egypt to refit or reorganize. There they would be able to defend Egypt against a possible attack by the Turks, who were now freed from any menace on the shores of the Dardanelles. The Dardanelles troops were, however, sorely depleted in numbers by disease and battle casualties and were hardly sufficient for the purpose; hence reinforcements were desirable and 31st Division was sent out (a) to supply the deficiency and (b) to form part of a general strategic reserve of troops for the whole Empire that General Sir Archibald Murray [C-in-C Egyptian Expeditionary Force] had been instructed to maintain. [It is a remarkable fact that, after suffering huge casualties during the fighting, the evacuation of Gallipoli was so well planned that it was achieved with almost no fatal casualties among the troops involved.]

Almost all the stores had been landed during the twenty-four hours we had been in harbour and once we had stepped onto the quay it was only a matter of minutes before we were en route for our camping ground. On the way we noticed with great interest the Gurkha sentries, whom we considered to be very smart little fellows in their khaki shorts. A mass of natives followed the column calling for 'baksheesh', which signified nothing to us and for all we knew it might have been a new kind of herb. We found out later that it meant a present of some kind, a tin of bully, a packet of cigarettes, or a piastre. [Piastra was the collective name given to any low value coin used in any of the Middle Eastern countries at this time and worth two pence.] Our first impression of these followers was not a good one since to our eyes they all

The port of El Kantara, with an Arab dhow in the foreground being unloaded, early 1916.

looked ragged and unwashed. For clothing they wore a strange collection of winding sheets which they had managed somehow to form into what looked like baggy trousers and a voluminous blouse.

The camp we occupied for one week was just outside the town, and not particularly clean, which meant that during our short stay here we did see a bewildering variety of insects. Christmas Day was an unusual experience for most of us, a broiling sun in the midst of winter upsetting all our ideas of the natural order of things. However, in spite of our novel surroundings, the cooks rose to the occasion and produced for our consumption certain birds which they said were turkeys. To begin with we thought they must have been dodos because, in spite of the most determined attacks with knives, bayonets, and even entrenching tools, they resisted all our attempts at dismemberment. Most of the men went into the town and had a rare old time. Some managed to make it back to the camp that night, others did not. They arrived in penny numbers throughout the day and were indisposed for some time afterwards. On Christmas night one of the men was, unfortunately, drowned in the harbour.

[This man was Private Arthur Berry aged 26, the son of James and Mary Berry, Lime Street, Cleckheaton. He is buried in the Port Said War Memorial Cemetery. He was to be the only fatal casualty sustained by the Battalion during their time in Egypt.]

A move by train was made on 29 December up the Suez Canal to El Kantara [Al Qantarah]. The line lay in between the Canal proper and the so-called Sweetwater Canal. Why Sweetwater? We never found out, it was much worse from every point of view than the Suez Canal water. [The 31st

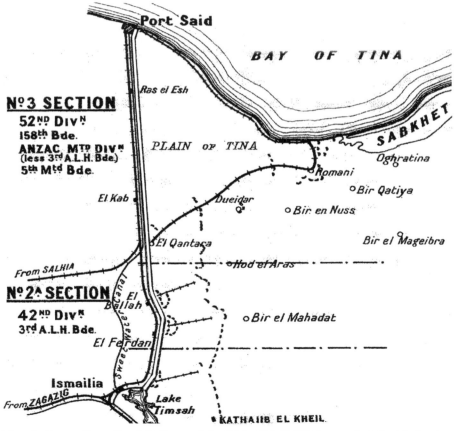

Map 1. Egypt: Suez Canal Defences, July 1916. 12th KOYLI occupied No 2A Section, December 1915–March 1916.

A small working party on the right and a narrow gauge railway engine await the delivery of railway lines at El Kantara.

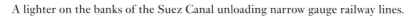

A lighter on the banks of the Suez Canal unloading narrow gauge railway lines.

Troops supervise the unloading of the narrow gauge railway lines.

On the left, narrow gauge railway lines are stacked on flat-bed railway trucks awaiting a locomotive to remove them.

A break from the work in the Canal Zone. The mood seems to be cheerful and the dress code appears to permit the wearing of football shirts.

Division took over the No 2A Section of the Suez Canal defensive line – See Map 1. This map was produced immediately after the 31st Division was replaced by the 42nd (East Lancashire) Division and shows the defensive structures built by the 31st Division, together with some of the railways and water supply routes the Division constructed.] The camp was pitched in some old defence works alongside the Canal, and that night proved to be the coldest that some of us had ever had the misfortune to experience. The next morning a platoon of D Company was detailed to escort a water carrying party of twenty camels and attendant natives to Hill 70, a small elevation in the desert five miles east of the Canal. The officer in command, being thoroughly convinced that a bold sortie into the heart of the enemy's country was about to be made, arranged his troops according to the best practice as set out in Field Service Regulations, and thus the little convoy somewhat gingerly proceeded. The arrival of an unknown general, and his snort of disgust on seeing the layout of the troops, caused the officer commanding the column some misgivings, but it was not until much later that he found that the nearest enemy force was at least a hundred miles away. Both C and D Companies under Major J.S. Charlesworth followed, marching through the great heat of noon, and officially took over the post from 18th Durham Light Infantry. The remainder of the Battalion (less the Transport, under Lieutenant W.S. Vincent) marched in on 31 December, and Hill 70 became our headquarters for a week or two.

Communications with Divisional Headquarters on the Canal was by overhead telephone line and we experienced a lot of trouble through the local Arabs cutting the wire. Curiously enough, we were never able to catch them in the act. The defence system was a central redoubt standing well up in the featureless desert, so affording a first-class target for enemy guns, but was surrounded by a cordon of outposts at various distances from 259–600 yards from the redoubt. One of the duties of the Orderly Officer was to visit these outposts at least once during the night. This was not a simple matter. There was no clearly defined path to follow, and one had to rely entirely on compass bearings. Even so, it was extremely difficult to find the posts. One officer (who shall be nameless) had the misfortune to lose his bearings altogether, with the result that he wandered about the desert the whole night closely followed by two Arab gentlemen who desired his money and his life but were kept at a respectful distance by the ostentatious display of his revolver (unloaded).

The majority of supplies would be delivered by small two-wheeled carts pulled by mules that were capable of carrying substantial loads on reasonably firm ground.

Immediately after arrival a small operation was undertaken by C Company, under the command of Major C.B. Charlesworth. This was the location and rescue of an aeroplane that had made a forced landing near Romani, about fifteen miles east of the Suez Canal. The work was successfully carried out in four days, though not without some loss of camel flesh amongst a ration carrying party under the command of Second Lieutenant P. Crowther, which set out to deliver supplies for the main body. The signallers on this occasion made great use of the heliograph; in fact, by its means almost constant communications was maintained between the rescue party and the headquarters in camp.

Marching during the heat of the day with full equipment was no joke. The sand gave way beneath the feet and those in the rear of the column were almost blinded and choked by the dust raised. History relates the following story, but not about one of our Battalion. In one particular unit, having marched thirty-seven miles in one day over the scorching desert, the men had almost reached exhaustion point when a halt was called and preparations made for a night's rest. Hardly had the weary soldiers thrown off their trappings when the commanding officer had them paraded and addressed them thus. 'Officers and men, I have just had a wireless message which states that we are at once to march the thirty-seven miles back to the Canal. Any man not capable of doing this step three paces forward.' Immediately the

This small convoy of carts is operating close to the Suez Canal; the building on the left also appears in the photograph on page 31.

The most efficient form of transport through the desert was the camel train. The eighth camel in this train appears to be carrying two very large objects.

The mood in this working group appears more serious and the majority of men to be older and possibly more experienced.

whole battalion stepped forward three paces, except a very small fellow in the very last Company. The Commanding Officer (CO) seeing this, rode up to him and, beaming with satisfaction at having discovered at least one real warrior in his command exclaimed, 'I'm glad to see there's one man in this battalion capable of this march, and I congratulate you'. To which the man replied, 'Don't be d – silly; I'm too blasted tired to step forward three paces.'

Life was not all beer and skittles in this country by any means. During the day the heat was intense but immediately after sunset the radiation from the sand was so rapid that within an hour it was bitterly cold, and continued so right up to sunrise. At 5 am, or thereabouts, the whole battalion stood to and shivered miserably on the parade ground until breakfast time at about 8 am, however, between 8.30 and 9am, the sun was well up and it was already quite hot. We were sorely troubled, though not very often, with awful sand storms, when scorching wind would suddenly arise, blowing the sand with

A closer view of the camel train suggests these containers may have been for water storage. However, had they been full of water it is doubtful the animal would have been able to stand.

Having reached their destination the camels expected to be fed and watered.

terrific force into eyes, nose, mouth and ears. It was quite impossible to breathe unless one had some sort of covering over the nostrils and the sand penetrated into every nook and cranny. Tents had to be sandbagged down, and animals and humans had merely to grin and bear the affliction until such time as it had passed away. The camels seemed to know hours beforehand when a storm was due, and they would turn themselves out of the wind, lie down, and refuse to budge until it was all over. When we were not working, or on parade, we would while away many hours by playing football – 'the Soccer code', as the sporting newspapers call it. We also spent much time searching the horizon with telescopes on the lookout for an enemy who never appeared. A far better instrument for this purpose, though, was the Barr and Stroud range-finder, which magnified up to something like 25 diameters.

[Barr and Stroud were professors of Engineering and Physics respectively at the Yorkshire College of Science, which became the University of Leeds in 1904.]

The lack of water was very trying. This essential liquid was brought to the camp daily by camel convoy; each camel carried two fantassis, rectangular copper vessels holding twelve gallons each. Occasionally, some visitor, generally lost or otherwise misguided, strayed into camp from the outside world bringing with him a few very small bottles of beer, and these sold for six shillings each! The allowance of washing water for each man was very small, and it was the usual practice for officers and men to use half the contents of their breakfast tea as shaving water. In consequence of this habit several of us developed a decidedly jaundiced complexion. The staple food of the army was, theoretically, bully and biscuits, and when all else failed these were always to be had. [Bully beef (corned beef) came in a small tin and huge quantities were produced by the Uruguayan company Fray Bentos. The product had first been used by the British Army during the Boer War. The biscuits were manufactured by Huntley and Palmer and their No 4 biscuit needed to be broken up and mixed with a liquid before it could be eaten. The biscuit was mainly used for emergencies.] It was surprising what a wonderful variety of dishes could be made from these two principal ingredients, and the authorities issued a booklet describing twenty or thirty recipes based on them. True, the biscuits were a trifle hard, but a prolonged soaking in water, tea or gravy at least rendered them edible. When we were at Hill 70, a consignment of biscuits arrived which gave us a mild shock.

A working camp out in the desert. Companies from 12th KOYLI were often sent into areas like this to build defensive positions.

They were packed in tins in the usual way, but instead of the ordinary square shape they were circular, about the size of a saucer. They were distinctly tough, and the only way to break them up was to strike them smartly on the edge with a sledge hammer. We did this, and out trotted a platoon of little insects! We were told that these biscuits were a surplus lot left over after the Boer War, but as rations were scarce they proved quite good eating after the insects had been shaken out! Very soon after our arrival at Hill 70, sundry officers appeared on parade garbed in the very latest things in light khaki drill. Opinion in the ranks, which was very audible at times, was somewhat divided as to whether it was any improvement on the old service dress.

The flora of the country was disappointing, but the fauna was present in inconceivable variety and numbers. Every known kind of beetle lived with us – every species of fly lived on us. By changing from tent to tent it was possible to acquire a different kind of flea every night. We made the acquaintance

Map 2. Egypt: Section Ballah-Ferdan showing some of the construction work done by 12th KOYLI

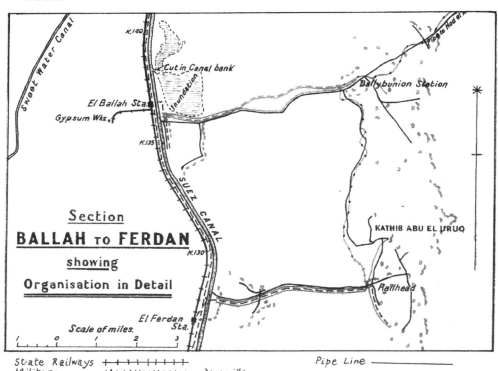

of chameleons, poisonous spiders, jerboas, lizards and prairie dogs. These dogs, which went about in packs like gangs of youths on a Sunday afternoon, became offensively noisy after sundown, and their dark masses were the cause of more than one alarm. On occasions they were hunted with gusto and 303 [rifle ammunition], chiefly when the OC Companies had been called away on business.

However, the real work of the Battalion consisted of the construction of a line of defence about seven or eight miles east of the Suez Canal, extending from the head of the Gulf of Suez to the Mediterranean Sea. The general scheme had been prepared with Lord Kitchener's personal approval and, as no Turkish attack on a great scale was to be feared, the scheme was rendered practicable [See Map 2]. Work began with every available man being put on the job, Companies moving out of the camp at 8 am and returning at 5 pm. The system was that of a strong outpost line, with posts half-a-mile to one mile apart; a front line, capable of withstanding an attack by heavy artillery, was connected by three communication trenches to a support trench about

Written on the back of this photograph is: 'Leaving Port Suez in tug boats to embark on the boat'. The large boat was the *Llandovery Castle*.

150 yards in the rear. The trenches were revetted [strengthened] and fire-stepped and a scheme of wiring was in preparation. On 9 January 1916, the first detachment left the Battalion for work as an independent unit and, from this time onwards until we left Egypt, the Battalion never again assembled as a complete unit. Ballah, El Ferdan, Hill 80, Hill 70, Ballybunnion, and many other places were visited at various times by large or small parties from the Battalion.

Early in February, Sir Archibald Murray, the Commander-in-Chief, Egyptian Expeditionary Force, informed the War Office that this defence scheme upon which we were engaged, was very wasteful in men and material, and he recommended an advance across the Sinai Peninsula towards the frontier. As a first step he proposed an advance to a suitable position east of Katia, twenty five miles from the Canal; and the construction of a railway to it. Katia was important because it was the only district in which any large enemy force could be collected within striking distance of the Canal, and it was there, and nowhere else, that shallow wells of brackish water were available. This plan was approved by the War Office and the construction of a standard gauge railway was therefore begun immediately, our Battalion taking a leading part in this work in addition to the building of roads and the laying of a water pipe-line, Second Lieutenant W.E. Oliver being placed in charge of laying the pipe-line. This work was steadily progressing when, owing to the military situation in France, the 31st Division was ordered to that theatre of war. The Battalion embarked at Port Said in the SS *Llandovery Castle* and sailed one evening at 9-30 pm. [Later, when sailing as a hospital ship, the SS *Llandovery Castle* was sunk by an enemy submarine on 27 June 1918. No date is given for the Battalion's departure from Egypt, but the 31st Division departed sometime between 1 and 6 March 1916, and was replaced by the 42nd (East Lancashire) Division.]

It has already been mentioned that we were part of a general strategic reserve in Egypt and in measure, as the re-equipping and refitting of the war worn troops from the Dardanelles progressed, this reserve could be drawn upon to meet the needs of other theatres of war, and this was exactly what had happened. An official account of the operations in the Sinai Peninsula says: 'The construction of the standard gauge line from Qantara [Kantara] to Haifa (412 miles from Qantara) was a remarkable achievement. Most difficult country had to be traversed. From Qantara to Bata there was nothing but desert … Water for the use of locomotives … was provided by a pipe-line system … capable of supplying 600,000 gallons per day. The furthest point from Qantara at which water was drawn for locomotives was at Kilometre 194.' It is interesting to note that the railway line referred to above eventually put Africa and Asia in direct communication, Cairo being linked for the first time with Jerusalem, Damascus, Aleppo, and other places.

The voyage to France was, comparatively speaking, uneventful; the tedium of sea, sea and still more sea – was somewhat relieved on passing the island of Pantelleria, sixty-two miles SW of Sicily, a huge mass of volcanic rock only forty five square miles in area, and rising from the bosom of the ocean to a height of 2,743 feet. We also sighted a whale or two, and saw them come to the surface to breathe when they spouted up a fountain of water in the process. Several sharks were also seen cruising round the ship; they had doubtless heard of the good food thrown overboard by our men for the first two days on the way out to Egypt! Submarines were as active as ever, and we steered the same erratic course as we did on the way out. The rule was, 'No smoking on deck after dark', but we have yet to discover why a cigar smoked on the saloon deck is any less visible than a cigarette smoked in the steerage. A formidable-looking naval gun was perched on the poop deck, and a naval gun team spent much time in polishing brass and peering out to sea. The alarm signal in case of submarine attack was three toots on the ship's siren, and we got a bad scare one drowsy afternoon when suddenly the siren blared out the dreaded signal. We needed no orders for all hands on deck and there was one headlong rush for the companionways, but we found that it was a practice call to find out if we knew our boat drill. For a time there was much confusion between starboard crews and port crews but, by the simple expedient of stowing surplus men away inside the boats, all appeared to be in order when the Captain came round.

Chapter 4

Arrival in France – Two days in the train – Hallencourt – March to Bus-lès-Artois – First view of the War – Preparation for the Big Push – The great attack of 1 July – Fearful losses of 31st Division – March to La Couture

I n the early morning of 8 March, our splendid ship steamed into Marseilles harbour and we felt that here at last we had really come to grips with the war on land. Egypt had seemed rather remote from the things that mattered and there was not a man amongst us who was not positively thirsting for blood and thunder. Later we got all we could desire of these last two aspects of war, indeed a little more than we had expected, perhaps. Almost immediately after the good ship *Llandovery Castle* had berthed, and to our great surprise and satisfaction, some Army Post Office men arrived with letters and parcels for us which, of course, were all addressed to Egypt. This we regarded as a great tribute to the efficiency of the postal authorities. Indeed, throughout the campaign one was frequently lost in admiration of this most necessary branch of the service, for the difficulties under which its work was carried out must have been immense.

We were forbidden the pleasure of landing, and spent a day leaning over the gunwales watching others work. At 9 am the next morning we were bundled into a train for an unknown destination; unknown at least to us, though no doubt the CO and the Adjutant had more of an idea than we had. For 48 hours we alternately dashed and crawled through 570 miles of French scenery, subsisting chiefly upon cigarettes and cold maconochie. [Machonochie: Tinned meat and vegetable stew sold under contract to the British Army throughout the war. It had a poor reputation amongst most British soldiers.] This was probably the most miserable journey that most of us had ever undertaken, or are likely to experience again. Up to this point all our moves and arrivals had taken place at the most inconsiderate hour of the day namely, at breakfast time and, true to our tradition, we trundled into Pont Remy at 8.30 am on 11 March. It was raining heavily and what with the wet and the wind, our empty insides and our ruffled tempers, we felt about as jolly as criminals on the way to the scaffold. However, in due course we found ourselves arranged in platoons and began a short march of six miles to Hallencourt, a small and pleasant market town of some 2,000 inhabitants, where we went into comfortable billets.

The population seemed glad to see us, and we were certainly glad to see them; for sixteen happy days we stayed here and really enjoyed ourselves. The linguists of the Battalion tried out their skills on the patient natives, who maintained their cheerful faces though they must have marvelled at our mutilation of their beautiful language in the process. It was found that the French language, as taught in English schools, was quite inadequate for the requirements of even the simplest conversation, but in the course of time a kind of lingua franca was evolved and by this means the bulk of the British army was able to make itself tolerably well understood. The French learned English very much quicker than we learned their tongue, perhaps because we had really not much time to spare for the subject. Almost as soon as we arrived we were served out with tin hats, the academic name for which is: steel helmet. For stopping bullets, and shell fragments travelling at relatively low velocities, they were most valuable and reduced the number of head wounds by more than half. The British soldier did not take to his tin hat at first, but he very soon realised its worth. They felt rather unwieldy before one got accustomed to them, and the general sensation was that of walking about with a large meat dish on the head. They gave us rather an incongruous appearance but, being made of manganese steel only 36/100s of an inch thick, they were comparatively light. Incidentally, it might be mentioned that they came in useful for other things besides head protection; they made capital wash bowls, dinner gongs and soup plates. Both the Boche and the French helmets were markedly inferior to the British, the German helmet especially cracked very easily when struck by a missile.

A rather large fly in the ointment took the form of physical jerks before breakfast every morning, and this brand of torture made us realize as never before what a terrible thing the war was. While here we perfected our arrangements prior to entering the war area proper. We were a matter of thirty-seven miles from the firing line, but we could hear quite plainly the distant rumble of the conflict raging to the east. One fine day we were issued with gas helmets – evil smelling, sticky things which nobody liked. They were a sort of Balaclava helmet of grey flannel with glass eye pieces, and we carried them in little water-proof pouches. In the event of a gas attack we were to fix the pouch on the chest so that the helmet could be quickly slipped over the head. So attired, we looked like a lot of inquisitors or members of the Klu Klux Klan. Gas helmet drill was added to the regime; when the Sergeant Major said 'One' all hands grabbed the helmet; 'Two', over the head; 'Three', the mouthpiece between the teeth, then we walked about to show how easy it all was, and gradually choked to death until the Sergeant Major said we could take them off.

At 9 am, 27 March, we said goodbye to the good people of Hallencourt and began our final march to the war. The first night was spent at Longprè, and successive nights at Vignacourt and Beauval (to be revisited later more than once). We came to rest at Bus-lès-Artois, where we lodged in low canvas-covered huts shaped exactly like rhubarb forcing sheds. They were planted in the midst of a small wood and were decorated on the outside with huge blobs of paint of various colours. Here we imagined ourselves to be perfectly safe and, as events turned out, so we were for all practical purposes.

On the day following our arrival, 31 March, the Battalion took over the improvement and upkeep of the roads in the divisional area, Captain H.F. Chadwick being placed in charge of the operations. On 8 April, we received orders which sent each company on detachment, which meant that we were to be detached from everything and everybody in the matters of pay and rations, but firmly reattached when anything disagreeable or hazardous was to be undertaken. The individual units of the Battalion were obliged to spend a very considerable portion of their time on this detachment business but, on the whole, we rather got to like it! Probably this was because there was only one commanding officer and one adjutant to each battalion, and neither could be in two places at once.

In accordance with these orders A Company (Captain J.C. Crawshaw) proceeded to Bertrancourt, 7,000 yards behind the front line, while C Company (Captain W. Cooper) went into billets in Colincamps, a small village only 4,000 yards from the firing line, but at that time full of inhabitants and comparatively undamaged. Each company was attached to a Field Company, RE, for work in the trenches making dugouts and general preparation for the big Somme offensive of 1 July 1916. B and D Companies, in the words of the Battalion War Diary, 'worked on roads and ponds'. In theory these were no doubt distinct, but in hard fact we found them practically identical, for the latter were choked up with mud and debris, whilst the former were inches deep in slush. Later, a party from D Company (Lieutenant R.E. England) reported to the Field Artillery before Colincamps for work on gun positions; here they expended much energy in digging large holes in the ground which, by order of the General Officer Commanding Royal Artillery (commonly known as CRA) were later filled up again, as they were in the wrong place!

At this period of the war, and on this front, it was not the practice to fire shells into enemy held villages which were close up to the line, to have done so would have made them uncomfortable to live in. In return for this consideration, the enemy refrained from dropping shells on our villages, and after the evening meal it was usual to stroll up and down the main street and listen to the war going on with great fury two and a half miles away. One interesting variant on the evening stroll was to climb the church tower and watch the enemy guns firing. By the means of a little gadget composed of a suitably ruled and scaled piece of wood and some pins, it was possible to mark down quite a number of enemy batteries, and the results were afterwards plotted on the map! Perhaps we ought to explain that the excessive humanity we displayed in thus leaving the opposite village in peace was not in accordance with our wishes; as a matter of fact we had no field gun ammunition to spare on chance targets, but the enemy did not know that of course. [Later in the war sound ranging equipment, consisting of a number of microphones were used to locate the exact position of the enemy's guns; the position would then be recorded on a map. When a large gun is fired, some of the propellant charge ignites in the barrel of the gun causing a brief flash to appear in the muzzle. Observers, using maps of the area, would then plot the location of the flash and, coupled with the information of the sound detectors, it was possible for the artillery to provide counter battery fire. This system was used by all armies during the war and with practice, and a sufficient number of guns, it proved to be most effective. Both sound and flash systems were being developed at the time Captain England was using his small wooden piece of equipment.] We have no means of telling who was first in the Battalion to make the acquaintance of a shell at close quarters, but the writer vividly recollects his first experience when one fine day a salvo of pip-squeaks [from a battery of German 77mm guns] arrived in the vicinity very unexpectedly. The main feeling was one of great curiosity and a sense of profound disappointment with the meagre result. He lived to revise this opinion very considerably, both curiosity and disappointment disappearing entirely.

We had not been long on the Western Front before we became acquainted with trench fever, a disease which was then little understood; in fact, for a long time its causes were something of a mystery, and men seized with it were recorded as having PUO which, being interpreted meant – pyrexia of uncertain origin. Sometimes they were labelled with rheumatism, or influenza, myelitis, and even lumbago! Advanced cases were diagnosed as DAH, meaning disordered action of the heart. The illness usually began with a bad headache and a feeling of great muscular exhaustion, and temperatures of 103 F [39 Centigrade] were common. Later on, intense boring and gnawing skin pains developed and became so unbearable that a patient could hardly bear the weight of the bedclothes. It was eventually found that the disease was primarily louse-borne, and that infection was caused by the excreta of the lice being blown about and lodging on the skin, finding its way into the blood via any small cut or abrasion. Conditions of life in the trenches made it very difficult to avoid contamination, and great numbers of men were evacuated to hospital with the disease.

By now aerial fighting had become general and about the middle of June we witnessed one tremendous battle between twenty or thirty British machines and a like number of Germans immediately above the trenches. For about twenty minutes these machines darted hither and thither like a crowd of swifts. They all kept up a constant machine gun fire, and both British and Germans in the trenches were so fascinated by the spectacle that the war on land temporarily stopped. No machine was brought down, but the Huns must have got the worst of the conflict since they made off and left the air to our own aviators. It is probably true to say that the aeroplane of the present day [1920s] owes its advanced position to the artificial stimulus provided by the war's demands. It may seem extraordinary, but it is nevertheless a fact, that in August 1914, 'aerial fighting was a problem which few could imagine taking place. All that was suggested, in regard to fighting, was that one airman might by swift manoeuvring pass across in front of an antagonist and seek to blow his machine over by the wind-draught from his propeller.' (C. Graham-White and H. Harper in *Aircraft in the Great War*.) Yet not two years later aeroplanes were dashing in scores about the skies and, far from being in danger of being blown over, were actually striving to get to close quarters with an opponent, the better to make him a present of a couple of hundred machine gun bullets. Our Royal Air Force [known as the Royal Flying Corps (RFC) between 1914 and 1 April 1918 when, it merged with the Royal Naval Air Service (RNAS) to form the Royal Air Force (RAF).] was a wonderful arm. It was impossible to regard these chaps with anything but hero-worship. By the end of 1916, so complete was their ascendancy over the German airmen that it was only occasionally that enemy machines flew over our lines during daylight. In fact, it was an event when they did so, and we found it interesting to watch them being shelled by our own anti-aircraft guns or 'Archies' as they were called, a nickname derived from a song popular when the war broke out: 'Archibald, certainly not', an allusion to the small number of hits made. An aeroplane two or three thousand feet high presents an exceedingly tiny target, and when it is travelling at about a hundred mph and altering course and height at the same time, it will be realised that more than ordinary skill is needed to bring one down. This was, however, occasionally accomplished, much to our gratification.

To give some idea of the extent to which flying developed let us consider a few figures. The Germans had in use in 1914 about 220 machines, 480 in 1915, but nearly 4,000 in 1918. They lost 2,000 machines during the war from various causes, and their casualties were about 6,000 killed, with just over 7,000 wounded and injured. The deadly nature of the occupation is shown by the similarity of the figures for killed and wounded. [Captain England's statistics have since been revised and recent estimates of British and German killed show the RFC/RAF lost 9,378 killed and the German air force 8,604.]

The village of Hébuterne was almost in the front line, and here we first made the acquaintance of the trench mortars, essentially trench warfare weapons. They threw large shells with a big explosive content and fairly accurately, and were especially useful for cutting wire or wrecking earthworks. When we first knew them they were very mobile, in fact one might say extremely so. The habit on both sides was to throw a dozen or so shells into the enemy trench and then, before he had time to retaliate, they moved to pastures new and were not in a position to be troubled by the artillery shells which the enemy chucked over to where he supposed the trench mortar to be. [The resident British infantrymen in such trenches very often cursed the trench mortar crews when the Germans retaliated with artillery or heavy mortar fire, the offending mortar men having long since gone.] On 6 May, the Battalion suffered its very first battle casualties, two men of A Company being wounded near Colincamps. On 10 June, all ranks were sorry to learn of the death in action of Private C. Newton, of C Company, the first member of the unit to give his life. Then in the first week of June we heard the astounding news of the death of Earl Kitchener. It is impossible to describe the dismay which this catastrophe produced in us, for we were men of 'Kitchener's Army'. The magic of his name had enthralled us, perhaps to a greater degree than it had others not so closely connected, and we felt that the man whom we could least afford to lose had gone from amongst us. The disaster was our sole topic of conversation for days, and we wondered how the nation could recover from such a blow. In spite of attacks on this great man that have appeared from time to time since the war ended, we can never forget the work he did. His self-imposed and colossal task was the transformation of the United Kingdom from a negligible factor into a military power of the very first rank whilst a titanic struggle was actually in progress, and complete success crowned his efforts. It was hard indeed that he should not live to see his 'new armies' prove their real worth. In accordance with the terms of a General Routine Order issued at the time, we wore black armlets for a period to commemorate the passing of our great leader. [Captain England's reaction to the death of Lord Kitchener is in strong contrast to that of most politicians and senior military commanders in Britain and France. By this time, June 1916, Kitchener had almost no influence on the conduct of the war at home or abroad.]

From the moment we landed in France we had been playing a small part in one vast scheme of preparation and training, whose object was a grand attack on the German positions in a desperate effort to end the demoralizing trench warfare; however, at the time we were completely unaware of any of this. About 20 June, the tempo of activity increased, with all units of the Division displaying their skill in every branch of military art. The companies of the Battalion were unceasingly employed upon the construction of new trenches, the reopening of those fallen derelict, the laying of light railways, the preparation of gun positions, the excavation of dugouts, and other innumerable tasks.

One day there was a great spy scare. It was alleged, and believed by some, that a civilian working in his fields on our side of the line had been caught signalling to his friends in the German lines. He had a couple of oxen, one white and one piebald, and it was supposed that by changing these animals about, according to a prearranged plan or code, he told the Germans all they wanted to know. One must be very credulous to believe such a story. It is pretty well agreed by connoisseurs in the art of espionage that, except in open warfare, signalling by an agent from, or close behind, the enemy lines is practically impossible, and in any case would be of little use as any information to be gained there is better obtained by other means. A spy's useful information is gleaned very much further back. It was understood that an attack was to be made somewhere about 28 June, and our plans appeared to have been well understood by the civil population and, alas, as we afterwards discovered, by the enemy too.

Feverish activity was the order of the day and, to our disgust, of the night also. Every officer and man was carefully and individually instructed in the part he was to take in the 'Big Push'; and the General Staff were indefatigable in freshening up one's drooping spirits by confident assurances that never before had they known the enemy to be so poorly equipped with artillery. We were destined to discover that never before had they been so well supplied. It will be helpful if we give a short explanation of the general plan for the great offensive of 1 July 1916, the actual date of the attack.

The German positions astride the Rivers Somme and Ancre were geographically strong, and had been rendered incredibly more so by German military skill: the enemy line was almost exactly that taken up in October

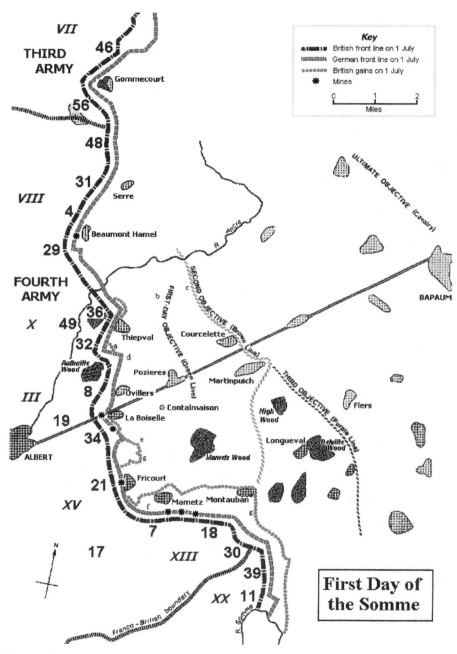

Map 3. First Day of the Somme Campaign, July 1916. 12th KOYLI's position can be seen to the west of Serre.

The original title of this photograph was 'Two of our opponents'. There is no proof that these two German soldiers were in the trenches near Serre in northern France but, the conditions would certainly be a contrast to Egypt.

1914 by the German Sixth Army after the battle of the Yser. Therefore, the Germans had ample time in which to develop their defences; and it must be admitted that they had wasted no time in doing so. The frontage selected for the assault extended from just north of Lihons, on the extreme right, to the Somme at Curlu, crossed the river then on to Maricourt (where the French and British Armies joined), thence by Fricourt and on to Beaumont Hamel and Serre, this village forming the northern end of the front to be attacked, though a couple of miles farther north a subsidiary attack was to be made by the Third Army (General Sir E. Allenby) against the salient at Gommecourt; the total frontage was just over twenty five miles.

The 31st Division (Fourth Army, General Sir H. Rawlinson) was selected for the post of honour in the operations, namely the holding of the left wing, the formation of a defensive flank and the capture of Serre. The Divisional front extended from St John's Copse on the left to Delauny Trench on the right, a distance of 1,200 yards; on our left was 4th Division. [St John Copse was the most northerly of four copses that were on or slightly behind 94 Brigade's front line, the others were also named after saints – St Luke, St Mark and St Matthew Copses.] During the night of 30 June, the assaulting troops moved into their assembly positions with remarkable success, the enemy displaying very little artillery activity. For the previous six days the entire enemy front and back areas had been subjected to an intense bombardment, in fact the artillery personnel engaged amounted to nearly half that of the infantry, and it was the general opinion that the enemy was more or less incapable of making any effective reply. There were others, however, who regarded this comparative silence as ominous; and they were right!

The morning of 1 July broke wonderfully fine and clear. Zero hour was timed for 7.30 am, and at that hour the valiant men of 93 and 94 Brigades advanced upon the formidable German positions in a series of waves, 92 Brigade being in reserve. At once a devastating fire broke out with fiendish ferocity over the whole of our front. A murderous barrage fire cut off the forward troops from those in the rear; scores of machine-guns poured their deadly hail upon our men, who nevertheless advanced line after line as steadily as though on parade, only to be positively mown down as by an invisible scythe. A and D Companies were attached respectively to 94 and 93 Brigades for special work on consolidation of captured trenches and construction of strong points. Both companies attempted to carry out their allotted tasks but suffered serious casualties in so doing. B and C Companies were assembled in the support trenches at the disposal of the divisional commander for carrying out constructional or fighting tasks as he might need them. Lieutenant J.S.L. Welch was killed at the head of his men, Second Lieutenant V. Mossop and Lieutenants H.D. Gaunt and J.T. Underhill were wounded and about 185 other ranks were killed and wounded, A Company, with 94 Brigade, alone losing 90 men. For gallantry in these operations Captain W.H. Roberts was later awarded the Italian Silver Medal for Valour, and Sergeant A. Adams the French Medaille Militaire. This was the first general action in which the Division had played a part, and it was in truth a ghastly baptism of fire. By 10 am that morning all momentum had been beaten out of our attack and as an effective fighting formation the 31st Division had ceased to exist. Our front and support lines

Map 4. The 31st Division's trench system facing Serre, 1 July 1916.

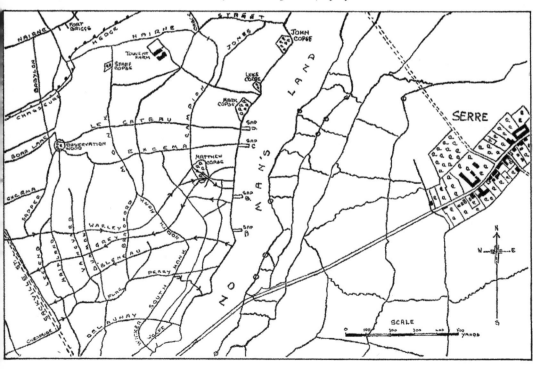

were pounded beyond recognition and 12th Battalion KOYLI, as the only unit in the front line approaching anything like completeness, found itself installed as the defender of that portion of the British front. Our men lay on the parapet along a wide trench of unsavoury memory known as Sackville Street, but our enemy had suffered as grievously as had his opponents and did not counter-attack. (See Map 4)

On the night of 1 July the remains of 93 and 94 Brigades were reorganised and took over the front line. On 2 July, the Battalion, acting as divisional reserve, withdrew to rear trenches and occupied itself day and night with the reconstruction of our battered defences, the location and salvation of the wounded who lay about the field in scores, and the burial of the dead. [The men of A Company, attached to 94 Brigade, had been in support of 12th York & Lancs (Sheffield Pals), 13th and 14th York & Lancs (1st and 2nd Barnsley Pals) and 11th East Lancashire Regiment (Accrington Pals). D Company, attached to 93 Brigade, was in support of 15th West Yorks (Leeds Pals) 16th & 18th West Yorks (Bradford Pals) and 18th Durham Light Infantry. The 31st Division's casualties numbered 1,349 killed, 2,169 wounded, 82 missing and prisoners; Total 3,600. [The 12th KOYLI War Diary for 1 July 1916 records. 'Molinghem 1/7/16. Battalion reassembled at assembly posts at 4.50 PM. Approximate casualty list 197 all ranks, including one officer killed and three wounded.]

In the late afternoon of 4 July, the Battalion left the trenches and marched, a sadder and wiser unit, to the old camp in Bus Wood. On 6 July, we were on the move again and started on a highly interesting march which occupied 18 days, our route being via Beauval (already mentioned), Prouville, Conteville (where we took train), to Berguette and Molinghem. Here Lieutenant Colonel Chambers was evacuated sick to England and the command passed to Major C.B. Charlesworth. Afterwards, we moved successively to Regnier le Clere, L'Epinette, la Fosse and La Couture, where we formally became part of First Army.

Chapter 5

Shelled out of La Couture – Preparation for the attack – The Fen district of Northern France – Guides – We move by train to Doullens – Sailly Dell – Awful condition of trench life – Expeditionary Canteen – Second attack on Serre

L a Couture had a small civil population and time passed pleasantly enough in our off-hours, but on the night of 30 July, the town [sic: in fact a village] was shelled for three uncomfortable hours. The following day heavy projectiles rained upon us for another four hours and it was unanimously agreed that the proper thing to do was an immediate transfer to a less dangerous locality. The move was therefore undertaken with remarkable speed and by 10 am, 2 August, the Battalion was snug and warm in a new area centred about Les Lobes. The company commanders at this time were: Captain G.M. Stockings, A Company: Captain D.E. Roberts, B Company; Captain W.H. Roberts, C Company; and Lieutenant R.E. England, D Company, with Captain W. Cooper as Adjutant in place of Captain S.Q. Newton, who had been evacuated to England sick.

Here we came across a battalion of those diminutive fellows known during the war as 'bantams'. None of them appeared to exceed five feet in height, and of course trenches constructed to suit men of average height were no good to them. A story which went the rounds concerned a veteran who had done his year in the line and was instructing a 'bantam' in his duties as sentry. 'You look over there', he said, '… thems the Germans, but don't you worry about them – they won't 'urt you. But keep your eye on those blinkin' rats or they'll have you by the leg and pull you off the bloomin' fire step in no time.' The rats certainly were a nuisance – until one got accustomed to them! With plenty of food and underground shelter to hand they multiplied exceedingly and grew very fat. So fat, indeed, that on several occasions we found it possible to trot along comfortably behind a crowd of them and

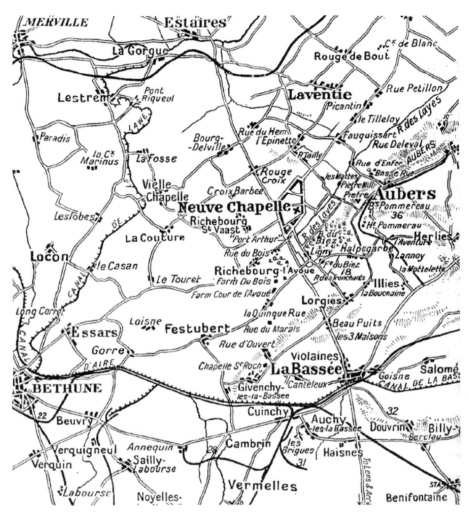

Map 5. Neuve Chapelle – Béthune area 1916 showing La Couture south west of Neuve Chapelle.

knock them down with sticks. They were huge things, as big as fair sized rabbits. Laying still in the dark damp dug-out it was possible to see the creatures running along the roof beams and peering down into the darkness and making horrid sniffling noises, just like a lot of small pigs. They were very bold too. They would coil up for the night on the pillow, inside the jacket or great-coat, and even get right inside the blankets. It was not exactly a nice sensation when one woke up to feel a furry mass moving round the feet, and it was even less pleasant when, having shifted the feet, the animal started to make frantic struggles to get out. Generally it was not alone in this, for the owner of the blankets was also engaged in a struggle to get out of them as quickly as possible. Very heavy rains always fetched hundreds of them above ground – flooded out and after a gas attack many hundreds would be found lying dead in the trenches and dugouts.

The vagaries of shells were always being discussed, and some strange results were observed in La Couture. The town was many miles away from the German heavy guns, and shells from howitzers descended at a very steep angle. It was said that one such shell cut a perfectly round hole in the guttering of a house, struck the edge of the pavement on the other side of the road and penetrated the ground immediately underneath a house where a dozen men were sleeping. Apparently it failed to explode even then, but the surrounding earth was fissured and cracked as by an earthquake. Another 8 inch shell fell onto a water-cart, complete with horse and driver, which was standing at the village cross roads: a terrific crash, a cloud of smoke and a rain of fragments flew everywhere; but when the din and dust had subsided, nothing remained to indicate what had so peacefully stood there but a few seconds before except for a little pool of water. A third heavy shell hit the church, completely demolishing a section of wall some thirty feet long but, strangely enough, a small centre portion to which was attached an enormous crucifix still remained upright and did so for two more years, although the town was heavily bombarded on many occasions.

All shells were given slang names derived from their chief characteristics. A 'Black Maria' was a very heavy projectile that on explosion threw out a huge cloud of dense black smoke. Forty feet of Mother Earth was the only sure protection against a direct hit by one of these. 'Coal Box' and 'Jack Johnson' were other names given to German heavy shells. A 'crump' was the German 5.9 inch shell, its explosion, when heard from a little distance, which was the most pleasant position from which to listen, sounded exactly like a long-drawn-out c-r-r-r-ump. It was quite a common shell and much dreaded, as its penetrative power was considerable; another name for it was 'five-nine', an allusion to the calibre. A very distasteful missile was the 'whiz-bang'. Its name explains its nature. It had a very powerful propelling charge and travelled through the air so quickly that all the indication one had of its approach was a vicious whizz followed instantly by the explosion. The phenomenon was due to the fact that the shell travelled quicker than sound, but nevertheless it did not travel as quickly as we did after the first one had arrived. [Both versions of Captain England's spelling of whizz are given.] The 'pip-squeak', already mentioned, was the common or garden 77 millimetre calibre German field gun shell, either high explosive or shrapnel. As shrapnel it caused us most concern. The most picturesque name of the lot was the 'woolly bear', a German shrapnel shell of large calibre that emitted at burst a big puff of brownish black smoke. [Another name for the German 5.9 inch shell.] 'Woolly bears' did great execution over our trenches on 1 July, 1916. Aeroplane bombs were known as 'eggs' and, unlike the curate's egg of tradition, they were always bad in every part. In fact, we loathed aeroplane bombs worse than anything else, although machine guns came a good second.

From the hour of landing up to the present time the Battalion had never worked together as a complete unit, except on rare and fleeting occasions, and it was during our stay in the La Couture district that our companies and platoons experienced the most extraordinary divisions and sub divisions. No task was so trivial but that a detachment of Pioneers could not be detailed for its accomplishment; no undertaking so important but that the ubiquitous Pioneers played their designated part. We had parties on canal work, maintenance of strong points, control of stores and ammunition dumps, timber felling, the laying and supervision of tramways, trench tunnelling (very difficult work, this), and on innumerable other jobs. It says much for the efficiency of the Quartermaster's department that even under the most exacting conditions rations never failed to arrive. It is also a remarkable tribute to the spirit of unity kept up by all the officers and men, and to the personal influence of Major Charlesworth, that the Battalion never lost its identity as a distinct unit, or allowed its splendid discipline to deteriorate in the slightest.

Battalion headquarters was set up at a farm down a quiet lane about a mile from Les Lobes and it was the duty of company commanders, and any others who had business there, to report to the farm at 9 am every morning. The Orderly Room was held in the courtyard, where a desk of sorts was rigged up in one corner at which sat the CO surrounded by his officers, but the tranquillity of the court was constantly upset by the antics of a frisky cockerel that persisted in running backwards and forwards underneath the bench uttering strange cries and getting in the way of the legs of the CO. Life was not particularly pleasant in those days, but there was one daily event which never failed to raise the spirits of the most despondent – the arrival of the mail meant news from home, from the wife, from the girl friend. The army mail bag was a most potent factor in keeping up the morale of men and officers, and what we would have done without our letters we don't know. No matter where we went, or how suddenly we moved, our correspondence very rarely went astray, though the same cannot be said of parcels, which very frequently arrived minus their contents. To us in the line this was particularly heart-breaking. These little gifts of food and clothes meant more to us than it is possible to express in words – they were links with home and reminded us, even when things were at their blackest, that somebody in Blighty was thinking of us, perhaps praying for us, and showing concern for our welfare in the most practical way they could.

On 27 August, preparations were being made for a local attack on the enemy's lines before Richebourg St. Vaast, and various detachments were lent to infantry formations to aid them in their work (See Map 5). By 13 September, however, the projected attack had been abandoned, and instead the Division extended its front on its right and took over the Festubert and Givenchy sections, one company of Pioneers being attached to each brigade and by 18 September these arrangements had been completed. The character of military operations was changed completely here. We were in what could be described as the Fen District of Northern France. The countryside was thickly covered with dykes (ditches), big and small, deep and shallow, and as the water level was only a few inches below the surface of the ground it was impossible to dig trenches as we knew them then. Instead of that, trenches, or rather breastworks, had to be built of tiers of sandbags about six feet high, and consequently they were easily damaged. One great advantage was that we enjoyed a comparative immunity from shell fire, at any rate in front and support lines, for the simple reason that the concussion from short-falling shells did almost as much damage to the enemy's defences as to our own. However, there were other drawbacks that were equally annoying. For instance, it was highly embarrassing when sheltering contentedly behind an apparently solid wall of English sandbags to observe a German bullet arrive with a slap on the rear wall of the so-called impenetrable defences; the reason being that, by some mistake on the part of the designer, the walls were only one sandbag thick instead of four and bullets passed through as easily as through butter. Again, owing to the complex plan of our entrenchments, it was never easy to be absolutely sure whether one was actually going or coming, that is, approaching or leaving the front line, consequently one strolled blissfully into all sorts of places that were under the enemy's observation. He hardly ever failed to respond to this kind of invitation, his usual method being to send half a dozen rifle grenades over. If the unwary victim failed to take immediate action a very sudden and unpleasant explosive shock could be the outcome. However, it was practically impossible to go over the top for short cuts, and that was something to be thankful for because there was no doubt that those same short cuts were nothing more or less than short cuts to paradise. At one time the Indian troops had held this part of the line and evidence of their occupation were all around. On the way to and from the trenches we had to pass through their cemeteries, which were particularly interesting since they consisted of a small collection of battered brick walls just behind the front line and were known as Indian Village. [The Indian Army's War Memorial to the missing is situated at Richebourg.]

The nature of our work made it necessary for us to move about the divisional area more than most other units; but to move about from place to place safely anywhere near the line, it was essential to have a very intimate knowledge of the neighbourhood. Obviously, we could not be expected to possess this knowledge for every part of the front and, therefore, when any work had to be done in any locality with which we were not familiar it was the custom for the Royal Engineers or the infantry to appoint a guide, who met our party at a pre-arranged spot and whose function it was to direct us to the scene of operations. However, we very quickly found that guides were to be divided into two classes: (a) those who did not know the way and said so before they started; and (b) those who did not know the way, but only said so when the column was nicely under fire and floundering about hopelessly lost. Hence, it became the practice for officers to survey the job beforehand and that was much more satisfactory from more than one point of view.

On 4 October 1916, the Battalion moved into a rest area near Béthune with Major H.F. Chadwick in command; Lieutenant Colonel Charlesworth having proceeded on leave on 24 September. Here we spent a day or two on company drill and general reorganisation and on 7 October three parties, each of two officers and a hundred ORs, proceeded to Lillers, Merville, and Berguette respectively, for duty at entraining stations. The following day the remainder of the Battalion moved to Lillers, where we entrained for a destination unknown, though rumour whispered Doullens, which meant Serre and Hébuterne again, and not a few prayed fervently that Dame Rumour might be hopelessly mistaken this time. It was, alas, too true; and in due course we alighted full of woe at Doullens and marched from there to Terramesnil, where Lieutenant Colonel Charlesworth rejoined us from leave. Whilst here the Transport Officer thought fit to allow a number of mistaken enthusiasts to be initiated into the art of mule riding. The animals were not provided with saddles and had only a single rein. All would have been well, comparatively speaking, had it not been for the callous behaviour of the Transport Officer, who incited the beasts to race madly across various fields of stubble with consequent disaster to most of the jockeys. After a day or so here we marched to a spot which we shall all remember for many years – Sailly Dell, a mile in the rear of Sailly-au-Bois, and thus only next door to our old friends Colincamps, Hébuterne and Serre; we had become, once again, a unit of the Fifth Army. [At noon on 3 July, during the battle of the Somme, VIII and X Corps had been removed from General Sir Henry Rawlinson's Fourth Army and transferred to the newly formed Reserve Army under the command of General Sir Hubert Gough. At the end of October 1916 the Reserve Army was renamed Fifth Army.]

Sailly Dell was a narrow chalk valley, and in the bottom was a tiny un-metalled country road also composed of chalk, the very worst material imaginable for carrying traffic. The rains had been continuous and heavy, the traffic likewise and as a result the road had become a sea of chalk mud, deep and affectionate since it clung to boots, clothes and equipment through thick and thin. On the steep valley sides we pitched our tents and daily performed miracles in defying the force of gravity. There were, of course, not enough tents to go round and the unlucky ones dug caves in the hill side. In six hours we had absolutely transformed the appearance of the

Dell, and the place positively bristled with weird and wonderful structures of all shapes and sizes, constructed principally of corrugated iron sheets, the origin of which it was not thought appropriate to be investigated. We did hear it said, however, that the Royal Engineers further down the road suspected some deficiency in their stocks the next morning, but very little credence was given to this unlikely story.

Once again the Battalion was split up into detachments, various parties moving into back and forward areas in the usual way. This was not the very best method of maintaining a spirit of unity, or for developing that elusive factor 'esprit de corps', the vitamins of military life. But thanks to the foundations laid in the early days by Lieutenant Colonel Dill and to the loyal co-operation of the men, we did manage to uphold the traditions of our regiment and make our name a synonym for good discipline and efficiency. For one who has had no experience of trench warfare it is impossible to imagine the awful conditions of life in the battle area. Almost all the fire trenches were more or less water-logged, and all the communication trenches were, without exception, inches deep in water and slimy, sticky mud. So much so that our men preferred to take their lives in their hands and make their way from point to point over the top. Carrying parties of all descriptions performed wonders under the most appalling conditions; it was not uncommon for men to be drowned in the mud and quite an ordinary thing to find one's comrades so engulfed in the stinking ooze that they had to be forcibly heaved out, leaving behind gum-boots, socks, and even trousers. On one occasion an officer of a neighbouring unit had the misfortune to find himself in such a quicksand of mud at a point where the trench side had been blown away; he was thus visible to the enemy, and was shot down during his frantic struggles to get free. When it is remembered that many of the communication trenches were over 1,000 yards in length, and that our men had to travel every yard carrying many pounds weight of military stores, with missiles of every description whizzing by and exploding with deafening crashes on every side, some slight idea – and only a very slight one – may be got of our daily and nightly life at this time. It was actually a relief to be allowed to remain more or less in the front or support lines rather than have to face the dreadful ordeal of a carrying party.

When we were out of the line living was not so bad. The Expeditionary Force Canteens were a tremendous boon and provided us with many luxuries which would otherwise have been unobtainable. To give an idea of what could be achieved under very favourable conditions, the following menu of an actual week is quoted; the gourmands were the officers of D Company whilst they were at Couin, and the mess was a canvas and corrugated iron shack in the middle of an orchard. This shack was later used by the Chaplain as a chapel.

BREAKFAST	LUNCH	TEA	DINNER
SUNDAY			
Sausage and Mash.	Sausage and mash	Tea, Bread and	Olives. Soup.
Marmalade.	Pancakes. Coffee	Butter. Jam.	Oyster Patties.
Bread. Butter.	Cheese. Bread. Port.		Roast Beef and Potatoes.
			Apple Fritters. Welsh
			Rarebit.
			Coffee.
MONDAY			
Porridge.	Irish Stew.	Tea, Bread and	Soup. Salmon.
Bacon and Eggs	Fruit Roly-poly.	Butter. Jam.	Cottage Pie. Rice.
Marmalade. Tea.	Cheese. Coffee.		Figs. Savoury.
			Coffee.
TUESDAY			
Shredded Wheat	Curry and Rice.	Tea, Bread and	Soup. Asparagus.
Bacon & Fried Bread.	Fruit. Jelly.	Butter. Jam.	Steak and Chips.
Marmalade. Coffee.	Cheese. Coffee.		Trifle. Devilled Sardines.
			Coffee. Liqueurs.
WEDNESDAY			
As Monday	Bully Rissoles.	Tea, Bread and	Soup. Sardines.
	Fruit and Custard.	Butter. Jam.	Tongue and Beans.
	Cheese. Coffee.	Lettuce & Radishes.	Devilled Almonds.
			Coffee.

BREAKFAST	LUNCH	TEA	DINNER
THURSDAY			
As Sunday	Boiled Beef & Onions. Jam and Bread Pudding. Cheese. Coffee.	Tea, Bread and Butter. Jam.	Soup. Prawns. Game. Blancmange and Fruit Paste on toast. Coffee.
FRIDAY			
Porridge. Bacon and Tomatoes Marmalade. Bread	Curry. Rice. Bread and Butter. Pudding. Cheese. Coffee.	Tea, Bread and Butter. Jam.	Olives. Soup. Sardine croquette. Roast Mutton. Jelly and Fruit. Coffee.
SATURDAY			
Shredded Wheat. Bacon & Mushrooms. Marmalade	Cold Bully. Potatoes and Pickles. Jam Tart. Cheese. Coffee.	Tea, Bread and Butter. Jam.	Soup. Lobster. Boiled Beef and Walnuts. Boiled Jam Roll. Savoury. Coffee.

To a student of cooking this menu will no doubt seem somewhat mixed, and it says much for our powers of digestion that we were able to do justice to the victuals. But it says more for the skill and resource of the mess cook that he was able to produce such appetising dishes from the poor materials at his disposal. Indeed, a good cook was a pearl beyond price and was carefully sheltered from the cold winds of the parade ground and the less exciting duties of military life such as rifle cleaning, kit inspections, and so on. The men did well, too, not so handsomely as did the officers perhaps, but nevertheless well, as the following menu card will show.

BREAKFAST	LUNCH	TEA
SUNDAY		
Fried bacon, bread and butter. Jam.	Sausage, mashed potatoes. bread.	Tea. biscuits, jam. Roly poly
MONDAY		
Sausage. tea. Bread. Jam, butter.	Rabbits. potatoes, Bread, rice pudding.	Tea. Bread and butter.
TUESDAY		
Rissoles of ?, tea, Bread, butter, jam, Or honey.	Bully beef stew, biscuits, 'spotted dog', cheese.	Tea, bread and jam.
WEDNESDAY		
Kippers, tea, bread, Butter, marmalade. and so on.	Sea pie, bread. Yorkshire pudding, treacle	Tea, bread. marmalade.

It will be noticed that rabbits figure in the menu here. These were fresh, or nearly so; at least not tinned, and GHQ [General Headquarters] sent forth a decree that for every rabbit issued a rabbit skin duly smoked and dried was to be delivered up in due course to the DAQMG [Deputy Assistant Quarter Master General]. Our consignment of skins was therefore dispatched, but shortly afterwards the Quartermaster was found sobbing with grief and it transpired that we were three skins short. Consternation reigned in the camp, and chits flew to and fro, but the loss was never made good, nor even solved, though the pioneer sergeant was observed to be wearing a pair of skin gloves which had never been seen prior to the issue of the rabbits.

The question will probably arise in the mind of the reader, from where did all this good fare come? The answer is to be found in the Expeditionary Force Canteens. These canteens were to be found in every town and in numerous villages all over the north of France. At them the soldier could buy cigars, cigarettes, chocolates and all kinds of canned goods duty free, and at prices far lower than those of the London shops; whisky, wines and beer were also obtainable for the officers' mess. The Department even took over French breweries, either wholly or in part, and brewed beer on the spot. In the course of time these canteens constituted the biggest shopping concern in the whole world, the average annual turnover being no less than £20,000,000. The stock sheets showed a total of nearly 3,500 different items; the tonnage handled was enormous – for example 12,000 tons during November, 1918. The great feature was that they served the fighting man first and the lines of communication man second. The canteens themselves were often worked in circumstances of great danger, and forward canteens were never withdrawn unless hostile fire became so intense that it was no longer practicable to carry on. The YMCA and the Church Army also provided canteens for the troops, though their buildings were more in the nature of recreation rooms and places for a quiet rest than mere shops. On general canteen work, the British YMCA spent no less than £21,900,000; of this, £17,300,000 represents refreshments sold.

On 22 October, preliminary orders for an attack on Serre, Beauregard and Miraumont were received, the role of the 31st Division being again, as on 1 July, to form a defensive left flank. Much work was done on trenches and dugouts. The weather at this time was atrocious and materials were exceedingly scarce. By 28 October, the proposed attack, in which A and C Companies were to be engaged, had been postponed no less than four times on account of the awful state of the ground. Two tanks were to work with the divisional troops, but it was quite evident that they would be quite useless under the prevailing conditions. [The first tank had gone into battle on the opening day of the battle of Flers-Courcelette, 15 September 1916, accompanied by two companies of 6th KOYLI.] On 3 November the attack was again postponed, and on the following day we heard that the operations had been put off sine die. The assault finally took place on 13 November and was successful, but our troops were heavily counter-attacked on the front and flanks and were compelled to withdraw because the troops on our right had failed to take Serre. The operation, however, served its purpose for by keeping the enemy in front of us fully occupied the troops further south were able to take and hold Beaumont Hamel, which was the main objective. The Battalion's casualties were light,

Lieutenant H.C. Williams and eleven ORs being wounded and one OR killed. Touching these operations, the following letter was received from the GOC 98 Brigade: 'The Brigadier has asked me to write and thank you for the great help your men rendered to this Brigade last night in bringing in wounded. From several sources he has heard of their good work and how extraordinarily hard they worked. He hopes that his thanks will be conveyed to the officers and men who volunteered last night.' The officers and men referred to were Second Lieutenant W. Collings and Second Lieutenant W.A. Hunter and seventy men of A Company. The first-named was later awarded the Military Cross for gallantry, while three of the rank and file, namely Sergeant A. Grace, Lance Corporal R. Metcalfe, and Private G. Hughes, received the Military Medal, and all deserved this recognition. It was about now that the Germans began the wholesale use of gas shells, and several of the men were unfortunately lost by this cause.

On 1 December, the Battalion moved with great thankfulness into a new camp, half a mile distant from the cave dwellings in the Dell. The strength of the Battalion was now twenty nine officers and 894 ORs, as compared with fifty officers and 988 ORs on the day of arrival at Hallencourt. About this time we received our box respirators, a great improvement on the flannel PH helmet. The box respirator was a rubber mask into which entered a flexible tube issuing from a metal container which held chemicals, through which the air was breathed. A mouthpiece was provided, and a good strong clip which took hold of the nose end like grim death. No one can say that they were comfortable, or even becoming, and the general feeling when wearing the outfit was that of being scientifically suffocated. However, they were quite efficient and saved thousands of lives. This British helmet was far and away better than that used by any other nation, and was proof against almost any gas which it was possible to employ in warfare.

Numerous parties, big and small, were occupied on tramways, roads, chalk quarrying, construction of dumps and refilling points, maintenance of trenches and erection of baths, cookhouses, horse lines, etc., etc. It has already been remarked that materials were somewhat scarce, and this passage from the Battalion War Diary is significant:

A permanent party of 18 men has been employed daily keeping the tramways in repair. IT HAS NOT BEEN POSSIBLE TO PROCEED WITH REPLACING WOOD RAILS BY STEEL ONES, AS NO BOLTS ARE AVAILABLE.

Christmas Day 1916 was, to put it mildly, rather cheerless. The GOC [General Officer Commanding] the 31st Division visited us during the morning and gave us a stirring address, after which we, in our turn, addressed with great success the Christmas puddings so kindly provided by a motherly Government. Truth to tell, the commissariat department of the British Army throughout the war was a constant source of wonder to us all and it is, of course, a matter of history how splendidly its work was carried on. We who were there and knew the fearful difficulties to be overcome cannot but acknowledge this, but it is nevertheless a fact that at the time we had many unkind things to say about this very department. As a matter of interest it may be mentioned that, while on the outbreak of war the Army Service Corps personnel numbered 498 officers and 5,933 ORs, and possessed only 248 lorries, yet on the day of the armistice these numbers had increased to the vast totals of 11,564, 314,824, and 86,837 respectively. In 1918, the daily feeding strength was no less than 5,000,000 men and 867,000 animals, the daily tonnage of foodstuffs 11,000 tons and of forage 8,000 tons.

Chapter 6

Move to Beauval – A miserable ten days. Aveluy Wood – In camp at Coigneux – Retirement of the Germans – Booby traps – We move north again. Battle of Arras (1917) – 'Sausages' – An audacious Hun – Construction of standard gauge railways – A thin time at Oppy Wood – High praise for the Battalion

From Christmas Day to 10 January 1917 the Battalion plodded steadily on with its various activities. In the New Year's Honours List of 1 January, the award of the Military Cross to Lieutenant P. C. Binns, and of the Distinguished Conduct Medal (DCM) to Lance Corporal Metcalfe were notified. On 11 January, we marched out of camp, or shall we say waded, en route to Beauval, where we went into tents. The camp consisted of one small hut about 10ft. x 6ft. in an advanced state of decomposition, intended as the officers' cookhouse, a pile of dirty tentage dumped down in six inches or so of mud, and a large marquee for the quartermaster's stores; a lucky man the quartermaster! It was dark by the time we got settled down, and then the question of food arose. We did the best we could under the circumstances and dined round the one and only fire in the camp; again in the quartermaster's stores. There was only one course, bully and biscuits. For the next ten days we were the most wretched gathering of humans in the entire British Army. The camp was a morass. Some of the tents were holey and rotten, and most were without floor boards. The weather was perfectly awful almost the whole of the time, and it rained hard and froze harder still alternately. To complete our discomfiture, fuel was scarce, and we were GHQ reserve, which meant that we were liable to be shifted at a moment's notice to any point on the front. It is a fact that blankets actually froze around one during sleep, and had to be forcibly removed by one's tent mates. The water stored outside in canvas buckets for washing purposes was daily covered with ice an inch thick, and to hear the first one up breaking this horrid crust with an entrenching tool caused one to shudder with fearful anticipation. We were vividly reminded of Napoleon's army during its miserable flight from Moscow, but we considered that if anything we were slightly the worse off. However, we lived through it, though we did lose some animals from exposure. Each day we managed to put in several hours of alleged training, and two of the officers were even so far removed from blank despair as to procure a portable cinematograph with which they gave performances in an adjoining estaminet at a charge of twenty centimes per head. We very much fear that the venture did not pay, but these budding film-producers eventually recovered the original cost of this equipment when the outfit was taken over by the Divisional headquarters. [The winter of 1916–1917 was one of the coldest on record at that time and, because of the lack of potatoes in Germany, this winter was known as 'the Turnip winter'.]

We moved to a delightful little place named Bernaville on 22 January 1917, and remained there until the morning of the 22 February. Generally speaking we had rather a good time at Bernaville, and managed one or two very successful sing songs in the parlour of the leading debit de boissons [a cafe where drinks could be bought – usually called an estaminet or bar]. These impromptu concerts were remarkable for the wonderful pianist produced by some other unit in the town. The Division was resting, but as usual the peaceful rest of the unfortunate Pioneer Battalion was curtailed and at 10.30 am on 5 February we proceeded (in the Army one never 'goes' or 'journeys' anywhere under any circumstances – all the best people 'proceed'); therefore we proceeded to a certain camp near Aveluy Wood, not far from Albert. Two companies were to work on roads and two companies were to labour in the wood itself.

It is, however, rather misleading to speak of working on roads, because, as a matter of fact, there weren't any. The entire area had been so hopelessly cut up by shell fire that it was absolutely impossible to see which was road and which wasn't, and it was, therefore, necessary to retrace one's steps to a spot where the road could be seen, take bearings from the map and thus mark out the approximate path the road should take. Trenches were then dug in suitable spots at right angles to this line, and the road located in this manner. The metalled surface was in some parts buried no less than six feet deep under assorted debris. I recall being sent to meet certain persons at the church in Thiepval and finding on arrival at the supposed spot nothing but a wilderness of mud and shell holes. A careful search revealed a hole larger than the rest in which was a peg marked, 'Church; site of!' By no exercise of the imagination could anyone possibly picture a large village as ever having stood there. One incident caused amusement. Thiepval was only a name, no trace of the village remained. The earth was shot to bits, and the shell holes were so numerous that for a couple of miles they touched all the way. Therefore, the accommodation at this salubrious spot could not be expected to be luxurious. It consisted of three stinking and battered German trenches, and half a dozen dugouts, mostly full of dead Huns and water. But one fine morning, to our astonishment, the smell of frying bacon was wafted along the breeze and we discovered that there was actually a Town Major for the place. There was no town, of course, but this was apparently of no importance; a town major was allowed for, and a town major there had to be. This unfortunate creature, who must have committed some dreadful crime, lived in one of the dugouts, and as far as could be ascertained his duties consisted of a rush at the double down his trench between shells to draw his rations, and a scoot back to his lair, there to remain until the next ration drawing period. The devastation in the whole of the area was complete and had to be seen to be realised. As far as the eye could see not a leaf of foliage was visible. Scattered groups of gaunt bare trunks of fantastic shapes a few feet high marked what had been beautiful woodland only six months before. Military equipment of every description lay on the ground in profusion.

The fighting line was some few miles ahead of us, but we occasionally came under desultory long range fire. The work in both Aveluy Wood and on the Thiepval-Pozières road was not without its dangers. The ground contained countless unexploded shells of all descriptions and one could never be certain that the next step, or the next blow of shovel or pick would not detonate some hidden missile – in fact, several of our men were wounded in this way. Our lot, as compared with those in the line was, however, luxurious and any slight mishaps of this description were treated very lightly. By this time night bombing raids by aeroplanes had become the fashion and though no bombs actually fell upon the camp, yet at times they were dropped sufficiently close to make life appear a very much over-rated pastime. Later on these bombing raids became very frequent, and in fact part of the game, but it cannot be said that they ever got to be enjoyable. There is something particularly hazardous about being bombed from the air. When the enemy is shelling a given spot, one does know with reasonable accuracy just about where the shells will fall and if possible the spot is avoided. But a bomb might fall anywhere to half a mile or so and yet be considered a rattling good shot. The only thing to do is to sit plump on the target and you are sure of never being hit. On the other hand, to sit on a target which is being shelled is disastrous, as it is pretty certain you will to be hit within a very short time.

So we continued with this work until 1 March, when we moved from Aveluy to a camp of Nissen huts near Coigneux, next to our old camp in Sailly Dell, where we rejoined the division which had returned to the front line. The War Diary says, 'Roads very bad, men marched well, no stragglers. Transport moved with great difficulty.' A Nissen hut, it should be explained, is a portable erection of corrugated steel bent into a semi-circular form, the invention of Lieutenant Colonel P.N. Nissen, RE. On our arrival at Coigneux we heard the glad news that the opposition had retired on a wide front – some even said as far as the Rhine! In reality he had merely begun a withdrawal to a formidable system of defences almost twenty miles in his rear known [to the British] as the Hindenburg Line. The reasons for this retirement were briefly, (a) our Somme offensive had shaken the enemy very seriously and had caused his defensive front in the vicinity of Arras to become a pronounced and dangerous salient; (b) an evacuation of the huge salient would significantly shorten his line, and thus release a number of divisions which could be moved into reserve.

As early as 17 February, in fact, it had become noticeable that the German defence on the British front was weakening and that his troops were being gradually withdrawn. The autumn had been exceptionally wet and had been succeeded by a long and intense frost, which had frozen the ground to a great depth – we made some experiments and found the depth to be at least 20 inches. A thaw began in the third week of February when the roads, disintegrated by the frost, broke up completely and the whole of the area of the 1916 Somme battlefield became a quagmire. The enemy, falling back over fresh unbroken ground, and favoured by a succession of misty days that covered his movements, retreated far more rapidly than we could keep up with him, and for some time we were completely out of touch with his troops. On the morning of 17 March a general advance was ordered by the British GHQ. At certain localities, where detachments of infantry and machine guns had been left to cover the retreat, there was little serious resistance to the advance, and that resistance was rapidly overcome. The evacuation was really a very astute move. We greatly rejoiced at the time, but afterwards we repented and wished he had done anything but retire. The net result was that the enemy now occupied new, clean and well-sighted trenches whilst we had to advance troops, guns and supplies over an indescribable surface. The Germans had destroyed everything they could and had cut down all cover of every description. The job of the moment was the reconstruction of roads and the Battalion devoted the greater part of its energy to the Sailly-Hébuterne-Serre road. Parties were also employed in the location and destruction of booby-traps, which will, perhaps, need some explaining.

Let us suppose that we enter a German dugout. A plain deal table occupies the centre of the space, and on it there is a book. You obey your natural impulse and pick up the book. Immediately there is a deafening crash and half the dugout collapses. Luckily, the entrance is not blocked and, half blinded by concussion and flying dirt, you rush out into the open air. You have miraculously escaped your first booby trap. Every imaginable device

This is all that remained of the village of Serre in May 1917, after the Germans had retreated to their newly constructed fortifications known to the British as the Hindenburg Line.

was used by the enemy in this way. A bayonet would be stuck in the ground, and its withdrawal would cause a violent explosion. To step on the stairway of a deep dugout was the signal for complete destruction of the shelter. In the course of time, however, we became wise to almost all these traps and there is no doubt that faulty fuses and hasty preparations rendered many of them innocuous. But while it lasted the experience was most unpleasant and after a heavy day of this kind one was almost afraid to lift knife and fork in one's own mess lest an upheaval occurred.

It was very interesting actually to travel over the ground which we had merely gazed at for so long, but even this had its melancholy aspect. Scores of British and German dead, principally on that awful 1 July 1916, lay about. The remains of many officers and men fallen on that fatal day were recognised and given decent burial. One party of the Battalion had a novel

A mine crater on the road between Arras and Bailleul. As they withdrew to the Hindenburg Line in 1917, the Germans used such methods to slow down the Allied advance.

experience when they discovered a German dugout crammed full of bottles of soda water. Ordinary water was scarce and had to be brought up by mule convoy, so our enterprising lads took possession of the Boche beverage and drank it, made tea with it, and even washed in soda water. The whole area was in an appalling state; dead of both sides lay everywhere, miles and miles of tangled and rusty barbed wire, rifles and equipment, rusty guns, piles of ammunition, battered trenches and derelict dugouts, a few broken down tanks, and over all hung that indescribable and unmistakable odour of putrefying flesh. As we surveyed the desolate scene we began to realise that the hell had not been all on one side of the line after all. The wonder was that the Hun had stuck it for so long. We had many different jobs to do, amongst others clearing a way through our old friend Hébuterne and making a corduroy road across No Man's Land in the direction of Serre, or rather where we imagined Serre to be, for the place was merely a mass of stinking shell holes, dead Germans, and lots of notice boards bearing trench names. Captain Chadwick set his heart on one of these and was just securing it when the retreating enemy opened fire on his late stronghold. Captain Chadwick had to make a dash for it, but nothing would induce him to abandon his notice board. Apparently the Germans were sending over all the shells they could not carry back, and we had some pretty thin times in and around Hébuterne.

At this time the enemy was using a very heavy shell against our aircraft. These missiles were of the usual time fuse type and travelled a great distance if they failed to explode high up in the air. One such shell landed by a group of our men on the Sailly-Hébuterne road, killing Sergeant M. Hudson and three men, all from A Company. These four brave soldiers now lie in the pretty little cemetery of Sailly-au-Bois, which is situated, as members of the Battalion will remember, almost in the centre of the village on the south side of the main street. When this cemetery was last seen by an officer of the Battalion in 1923, it was a perfect blaze of colour and was really wonderfully kept. Even at that time there were still hundreds of graves without their official headstones, having instead the wooden crosses erected by the unit at the time of burial, and it is a remarkable fact that of all such battalion crosses those made and erected by our own pioneers section appeared to have best stood the test of time. [The cemetery at Sailly-au-Bois contains eight

KOYLI graves and of these four, Sergeant. M. Hudson, Lance Corporal. J.J. Gardner, Private. P Murray and Private A. Whitaker, have the same date of death, 3 March 1917 and must, therefore, be the ones referred to by Captain England. Only one has his home town recorded: Private. P. Murray, aged 19, of Gateshead on Tyne.]

A date of importance to us was 8 March 1917, when the Battalion completed one year's service in France. Work of various kinds was carried on until 19 March, when we marched to Thièvres, then on to Bonnieres the following day and arrived in Héricourt on 21 March. These moves were rather enjoyable affairs, all things considered. An average day's march was twelve or thirteen miles, but on occasions we did more – once marching eighteen miles in full marching order without a man falling out. As regards billeting arrangements, the first method we adopted was to march en masse into the village or town and then moon about until billets had been found and allotted. But after a little experience of this, we hit on a far better system. An officer or two and an NCO from each company set off on bicycles ahead of the main body. On arrival at the appointed village the Town Major was aroused from sleep and the impending arrival of the Battalion reported to the astonished official. Then the billets were inspected and assigned to companies, each NCO being told exactly where his company was to go and, as soon as the Battalion approached, these NCOs met their respective companies and guided them straight to their quarters, thus avoiding any delay. The billeting officer himself pointed out to the officers their quarters and messes, and the whole system worked splendidly. After arrival the first thing to do was to get a meal ready and when this was over we were generally free to do whatever we pleased for the remainder of the evening. Usually we gathered together in the principal estaminet, sampled the good vin blanc, which was very cheap and very vinegary, and played cards. Poker, whiskey poker and vingt-et-un were the chief games, but we believe the highbrows in HQ Mess actually made a habit of playing bridge.

On 22 March we marched to Tangry, where we rested over night before moving on to Febvin Palfart and eventually to St. Floris, where we remained for a time. This was a nice little village a few miles from St. Venant, a town well known to troops because of the convent, where the kind nuns provided baths for weary soldiers. For three days we basked in the peaceful atmosphere

This is the village church in Sailly-au-Bois (1922). Sergeant M. Hudson, Lance Corporal
J.T. Gardiner and Private P. Murray of A Company, were killed on the Sailly-Hébuterne
road, and are buried in the church yard.

of St. Floris and the war seemed very distant; not even an aeroplane soared above to remind us of the struggle raging a few miles away. Alas, we were not to enjoy this for long for once again our well earned rest was curtailed and on 1 April the detachment business began again, C and D Companies marching via Maisnil-lès-Ruitz to Bray, where they came under the jurisdiction of the CRE (Commander Royal Engineers) XVII Corps.

As these two companies arrived on the camping ground, which was merely a hill side covered with young trees, snow began to fall and they had to pitch camp and cook food in a blizzard. To make matters worse the ASC had forgotten that man shall not live by bread alone and all they could offer us were a few small loaves. Captain Chadwick immediately exclaiming, 'What are these among so many', or words to that effect, dashed off on horseback to Corps HQ and gave them such a mauvais quatre d'heure that plenty of rations were brought up at the gallop within half an hour. The remainder of the Battalion moved on 8 April, to Le Hamel, a few parties having previously left for various destinations. No sooner had they nicely settled at Le Hamel than they were shifted on to St. Aubin by bus, an awful ordeal calculated to destroy any but the soundest of livers. C and D Companies rejoined from Bray on 10 April, and the Battalion was once again more or less complete.

It is necessary here to explain why we were in this area and the events leading up to the battle of Arras. At the close of 1916, a general plan had been agreed upon by all the Allies to conduct a simultaneous offensive on all fronts and the role of First Army (General Sir H.S. Horne with 1st, 2nd, 3rd and 4th Canadian Divisions, and 13 Brigade, 5th Division) in the scheme was to secure the left flank of the British operations by seizing Vimy Ridge, a geographical feature of immense importance which, rising to a height of 475 feet, dominates the country in every direction. The task of the British was to attract as large forces of the enemy as possible, thereby reducing the opposition to the French further south who were in a very exhausted condition. The preparations for a big offensive of this kind are long and arduous. The front selected for the attack, nearly fifteen miles in length, was served by only two single railway lines leading to Arras, the combined capacity of which was less than half the requirements. It is laid down in Imperial Strategy (1906) that 'Railways are the arteries of modern armies. Vitality decreases when they are blocked and ceases when they are permanently severed.' Much constructional work, therefore, of both standard and narrow gauge railway had to be undertaken and it was for this purpose that we had moved into the battle area.

The attack was launched at 5.30 am, 9 April 1917. Our infantry's advance was everywhere so irresistible that within forty minutes the whole of the German first line system had been stormed and captured, in spite of heavy squalls of snow and rain. In this battle a greater mass of artillery, both guns and howitzers, was used for the initial bombardment of the enemy positions than had yet been available in any previous British attack; the actual numbers were 989 heavy guns and 1,890 field pieces. For three weeks before the attack all these guns had been continually bombarding the German forward and back areas. In order to get the best possible results from this great weight of metal that was daily being hurled into the enemy lines, the artillery made great use of aeroplanes and large numbers of kite balloons; the Tommys called them 'sausages' because they were just that shape. They were also used for general observation and were controlled by power winches mounted on motor lorries. The enemy did not seem to have as many as we had; indeed, at some places the British balloons appeared to hang in the air as thick as grapes. It was most annoying, and nerve racking, to have a Hun balloon suspended opposite our positions knowing, as we did, that every little movement was observed. For a long time the only method of bringing one down was to send out an aeroplane which pumped many rounds of incendiary bullets into the craft. When attacked in this manner the observers, in the car of the balloon, strapped on their parachutes and leapt into the air. If the attacking plane was particularly vindictive it cruised round and round the falling parachutists and pumped bullets into them as well. We saw this done on several occasions. Later, long-range shrapnel was used to bring down these balloons and we seemed to be more successful at this than did the enemy. In the course of the war the German losses of balloons were about 600, 80 per cent of these being by aeroplane attack. In fact, the balloonist's lot was, like the policeman's, [in the Gilbert and Sullivan operetta] 'not a happy one'; he was not armed and simply hung there to be shot at.

It was obvious, even to us, that a very extraordinary mass of artillery was engaged, for the whole district seemed to be covered with gun positions and if the enemy had done any shelling worth talking about he would have found it difficult to miss these choice targets. There was no attempt at concealment, the number of guns was too great for that. Our aircraft did all that was necessary in keeping hostile planes away and only very occasionally did we see one over our lines. [April 1917 became known as 'Bloody April'. The RFC losses far exceeded those of the Germans, partly because the German aircraft rarely crossed the British lines choosing to fight over their own territory, and partly because at this stage in the war they had superior machines.] It is worth noting that the Battle of Arras was the first occasion during the war when a form of unity of command with the French forces was attempted; the British troops were placed, within certain limitations, under the control of General Robert Nivelle. [In January 1917, the British Prime Minister, David Lloyd George, had attempted to place the whole of the BEF under the command of the new French C-in-C, General Nivelle, who had successfully attacked the Germans at Verdun. Relations between Lloyd George and Field Marshal Sir Douglas Haig, C-in-C of the BEF, became very strained. Haig was vindicated when Nivelle's great attack along the Chemin des Dames failed to live up to expectations, leading to mutinies in the French Army. Nivelle was quickly dismissed.]

On 12 April, the fourth day of the attack, we began work on the Fond du Vase standard gauge railway, and very good progress was made with little interruption from enemy fire. On 28 April, D Company moved to a camp just behind Écurie, and on 30 April, as the offensive had become less intense, there was no longer any need for our services, the whole Battalion moved to two new camps amongst the old trenches to the east of Arras. The 31st Division had meanwhile arrived at Roclincourt and taken over the front line.

The weather was now perfect and ideal for aerial work and scores and scores of friendly and enemy craft flew about the skies day and night. Our particular German plane used to come down very low, only thirty or forty feet from the ground, and pour a hail of machine gun bullets on anything that took the fancy of the pilot. This occurred on several occasions, but the audacious Hun was guilty of an error of judgement when he picked out the Nissen hut occupied by the Divisional general and put half a dozen bullets through his bed! The next night there was a tank waiting at the particular crossroads most favoured by the aeroplane and when he started his little game the tank also commenced to play a tune on him with the result that he came with a crash to earth and was consumed in flames. It was whilst we were here that we witnessed a very fine spectacle in the form of an ammunition dump on fire. Near Arras station were stored many, many tons of explosives of all kinds and one afternoon fire broke out. Hundreds of horses stampeded out of the town and up the road past our camp, a column of dense smoke rose into the air a couple of hundred feet in height, the pitter-patter of thousands of rounds of small arms ammunition was varied with the occasional roar of big shells as they exploded and every now and then clouds of coloured rockets shot up. German aeroplanes sailed over to enquire into the matter and were so interested that they forgot to drop any bombs; all railway traffic through Arras was stopped and the display continued through the night and well on into the next day. We heard afterwards that the outbreak was caused by the guards lighting a fire in a little hut formed from boxes of ammunition; as it would not burn up these intelligent warriors poured petrol over their weak flame and the result was an immediate journey to Paradise for all of them and the destruction of a million pounds worth of ammunition.

As previously mentioned, the French were to launch their offensive on the Aisne at the same time as the British attacked Vimy, but owing to very bad weather they had to postpone it until 19 April. Unfortunately, it was a failure and, by request of the French High Command, the British continued offensive operations on the Arras-Vimy front with the object of absorbing the enemy's reserves. Accordingly, the Battalion took part in preparing trenches before the villages of Oppy and Gavrelle as a jumping-off place for a new attack and we were destined to experience a pretty rough time for a few weeks. It was wholly night work and the four mile journey from camp to the front line, across a bare and fire-swept plain, was a trifle hair-raising. At about this time we learnt with very deep regret of the death on our front of Lieutenant P. Crowther; he had transferred to the Royal Engineers where his civil engineering experience could be best utilised, and it was while in command of a wiring party that he met his death.

An attack by 92 and 93 Brigades was delivered against Oppy Wood and village on 3 May, A and C Companies being attached for the consolidation of captured positions (see Map 6). The assembly trenches were very poor affairs indeed, and just as the infantry and our men were taking up their positions in the darkness the enemy opened a very heavy artillery and machine gun

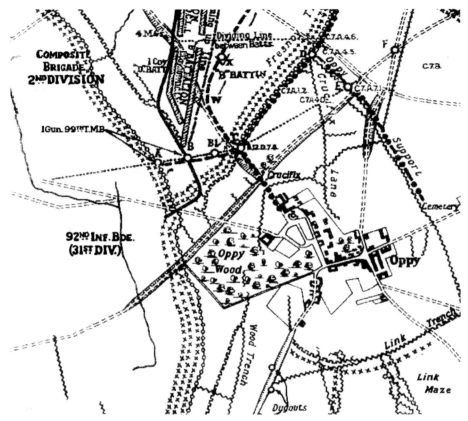

Map 6. Oppy Wood.

fire upon us. The attack, when delivered, was unsuccessful, and the two companies, having suffered many casualties, returned to camp the next day. A period of very difficult work on the front line before Oppy followed, during which Major Stockings and Captain D.E. Roberts were conspicuous. The latter was awarded the Military Cross for handling his command with great skill and coolness in a difficult situation on the night of the 14/15 May, when all his officers had become casualties. Work on the front line continued until 18 May, and the next day the Division handed over to 63rd (Royal Naval) Division, and, on 20 May, the Battalion, less A Company, marched back to a camp not far from Maison Blanche, on the main road from La Targette to Écurie; A Company were half a mile away to the south. From here B and C Companies were working on the roads to the north and south respectively of Farbus Wood. A Company were doing various odd jobs under the 226th Field Company, Royal Engineers, and D Company worked on the western half of the Thelus-Farbus road. It is interesting to note here that while on the outbreak of war the Corps of RE consisted of 1,831 officers and 24,172 ORs, in November, 1918 there were 17,711 officers and 322,739 men.

On 31 May, A Company began preliminary work for the construction of a light railway just below Roclincourt. Throughout the month of June the Battalion was engaged on various tasks, which it completed with its usual efficiency. Towards the end of the month 94 Brigade attacked the enemy lines at Gavrelle with complete success, B and D Companies, under Captain D.E. Roberts, being attached to open up communications. On the night 28/29 June these two companies dug a trench 360 yards long, 4½ feet deep and 3 feet wide and were specially congratulated by the GOC 94 Brigade; casualties numbered thirty-nine. Lieutenant Colonel W.B. Hulke, 14th Yorks & Lancs, (2nd Barnsley Pals) writing to 94 Brigade Commander said, referring to our work,

> I went round my whole front this afternoon and I would like to bring to the Brigadier's notice, if I may, our appreciation of the excellent work performed last night by the K.O.Yorks. L. Inf. in digging the new communication trench between Railway and Cadorna... I am of the opinion that these Companies should be specially commended for their work in view of the fact that shortly before zero they suffered heavy casualties. In spite of this they commenced work before dusk.

Again, the GOC 94 Brigade, (Brigadier General G. Carter-Campbell), writing to our CO, said, 'I have myself seen this trench and can corroborate all he says. These companies did most excellent work, not only on the night of the operations, but on the previous night also and I hope you will let it be known how all ranks of my Brigade appreciate the same.'

Corporal Hirst, Lance Corporal Wright and Private Parkinson were all awarded the Military Medal for their splendid example and gallantry on this occasion.

Chapter 7

We leave France for Flanders – Work on light railways – Great attack on Passchendaele – Terrible conditions in the Ypres Salient, 'Elephants Blood', Honours and Awards

O n 1 July 1917, a melancholy anniversary, the Battalion once more left the 31st Division, marched to Maroeuil and there entrained for Hopoutre, near Poperinghe, where it arrived at 9 am on the following day. [Hopoutre was a newly constructed military railway station on the south-eastern edge of Poperinghe. It has been suggested that the name was a pun invented by the British soldiers and could be interpreted as 'Hop out'.] Thus for the first time we set foot in Belgium; poor little Belgium. Her appalling sufferings at the hands of the German hordes, and the unique example set by her heroic King, Albert I, will never be forgotten.

The CO was without instructions, and billeted his men in Poperinghe itself. Dear old Poperinghe, affectionately known to the whole of the British army as 'Pop', the little war-swept town to which so many thousands of weary khaki lads marched seeking a little rest, a little change from the stinking, mud filled Ypres salient. The reason for our moving north was that we were to be lent to the Fifth Army for special work on railways in connection with that superhuman effort which has gone down in history as the attack on the Passchendaele Ridge, the object of which attack was the seizure of the high ground to the north and the north-east of Ypres. Under the 2nd Battalion, Canadian Railway Troops, we spent a month here practising the rapid laying of light railways, what we called 'Decauville track'. [These were pre-fabricated sections of narrow gauge track that could be quickly attached to steel sleepers. Named after a French railway engineer, extensive use was made of it during the war by British and French engineers. The Germans had a similar system in operation.] The weather was beautiful, the sun shone brilliantly, the birds sang, we had plenty of tents and plenty

A general view of Ypres take in the last year of the war, showing the remains of the famous Cloth Hall and the surrounding devastation.

of good food, and it all seemed like a glorious picnic. Sadly and too soon, came the awakening. On 29 July we began work in earnest as our part in the extremely arduous preparations for the great attack. The infantry advanced to the assault on 31 July 1917 over an appalling surface and our task was to lay these light railways to selected tactical points where ammunition and food dumps would be set up in the wake of the advance; all the work being done under fire which was very often intense. There was every prospect of a splendid victory when Fate blundered in.

Rain fell in torrents in the late afternoon of the first day and continued without cessation for four days and several days after that the weather was most unsettled. The low-lying clay soil, pitted with shell holes, became a succession of muddy pools, and the valleys became impassable except at a few points. This effectively slowed down our advance to a crawl, gave the enemy time to recover from his defeat of 31 July, and allowed him to bring up reinforcements. The Battalion, however, had no time on its hands, and under frightful conditions we went on laying down a regular network of lines to batteries and dumps over which many tons of ammunition and supplies were transported, more than 18,000 tons being brought up in one week alone. Much to the regret of everyone, our CO, Lieutenant Colonel E.L. Chambers, who had proceeded to England on 11 August, was struck off the establishment of the Battalion on being posted to a Training Reserve Battalion in England. Major C. B. Charlesworth took command and was promoted to the rank of lieutenant colonel on 23 September 1917 and became our fourth commanding officer.

The British attack was resumed on 16 August [the attack on Langemarck], but little progress was made. At the few points where we did advance the Battalion's job was again the construction of light railways. The weather broke again and continued wretched until the end of August. The ground became absolutely water-logged, so that any fresh infantry advance was out of the question. We, of course, found plenty to do in the maintenance of our railways, for the enemy spared no effort to shell them to bits, and the Battalion really had a very trying time indeed. Casualties were continuous, in fact it was roughly calculated that the average effective life of a soldier in the sector was about three days! Even when out of the line or off works we had no rest for, no matter where we moved, we were both bombed and shelled, and between the 16 and 20 August we lost fifteen ORs killed and wounded from this cause alone. [Captain England does not reveal who calculated that, 'the effective life of a soldier in this sector was about three days', but it can be taken as a measure of what the ordinary soldier believed the casualty rate to be during this battle.]

Being bombed by aircraft was not a pleasant experience by any means, but we always found a peculiar fascination in watching the nocturnal evolutions of the big bombing planes, like so many huge white moths as they flew in and out of the searchlight beams. We were delighted when we observed our shells bursting closer and closer, until at last a machine was hit. How we cheered to see the frail craft come crashing down to earth, never a bit of pity for the poor doomed humans inside. And, after all, why should we pity them for they had little enough for us as they dropped their 300 kilogram 'eggs' upon us. These particular bombs contained a charge of 180 kilograms of amatol which, when they burst made a frightful mess of things for a fair distance around. Therefore nobody enjoyed having one explode nearby.

The first half of September was bright and dry, so it was decided to renew the British attack on 20 September. Meanwhile all the energies of the Battalion were devoted to laying down our precious Decauville track, the sight of which we had come to hate with a deadly hatred. As the momentum of our attack gradually declined, so the call on pioneers grew less, and the other pioneer battalions who were working in the sector were gradually withdrawn until, as Lieutenant Colonel C.B. Charlesworth so expressively puts it in his diary, '...we found ourselves the only pioneer battalion left in that plague-stricken spot, and only half of the Canadian Railway Troops. We also found out the reason for this. We had been specially asked for because of the excellent work our men had done.' Lieutenant Colonel Charlesworth also expressed the opinion that '...the only reward in the army for good work was to be immediately put on to another job rather more fierce than the first one' and, indeed, it seemed to be so. During the month we received a large number of reinforcements, including 250 men transferred from the Royal Engineers, and at one time we were no less than 1,300 strong, with forty officers, a very big command in the field. It was a very lucky circumstance that at this most strenuous period we had plenty of officers and men to ensure a certain amount of comparative rest for everyone.

On 20 September, as arranged, the attack was renewed with great success [Battle of the Menin Road]. On 26 September a further small advance was made with equally brilliant results [Battle of Polygon Wood], and here a halt was called until 4 October, for which date an important operation was planned. The Battalion carried on with the good work of keeping the light railways in working order, no light task, as the track mileage was considerable. Most of it was under direct enemy observation, and he certainly did his best to blow it to Jericho; in fact, a lot of it did go there but, as soon as darkness fell, off we went with heavy feet and heavier hearts to repair the damage. The continuance of the operations depended on these light railways because without food and ammunition troops cannot fight and as the roads were not roads any longer the only channels of communication with the line and the batteries were these railways.

The attack fixed for 4 October [Battle of Broodseinde] duly took place and splendid results were achieved, in spite of a severe gale and the accompanying torrents of rain. On the night of 3 October Captain H.D. Gaunt and three of his men were wounded on the Forest Hall line. But, in spite of the great British achievements and the long period during which active operations had been going on, the work had in reality only just begun. Houthulst Forest, 'the key to Flanders', as the great Duke of Marlborough called it, together with the high ground beyond, was still in the enemy's hands and it was essential, if at all possible, to capture both before winter set in. Accordingly, more light railways had to be laid and existing ones kept open to traffic. An attack was delivered on 9 October [Battle of Poelcappelle] and another three days later [attack on Passchendaele]. In support of these offensives, great quantities of supplies and ammunition passed over our railway lines, a fact of which the observant Hun was well aware. Nor did he lose any time in letting us know it, for on 16 October Second Lieutenant L.H. Bingham was wounded.

The ground was now in such a state that any movement was a great physical effort. Sir Douglas Haig in his dispatch wrote that 'the state of the ground, in consequence of rain and shelling combined, made movement inconceivably difficult … it was still the difficulty of movement far more than hostile resistance which continued to limit our progress'. The entire area was a sea of filthy, slimy, stinking mud; so bad, indeed, that percussion fuse shells merely buried themselves in the swamp and exploded comparatively harmlessly. Animals and men were drowned in it; rifles were dropped never to be seen again. It was absolutely fearful and how men could survive the terrible ordeal is difficult to understand. Captain P.C. Binns and three of his Company were wounded on 29 October. For the whole month the casualties were eight ORs killed and three officers and thirty ORs wounded. The total is not formidable, but that was only because we seemed to be under the special protection of Providence. If casualties had been in proportion to the weight of metal hurled in our direction, then the total should have been more like a hundred killed. But it was very noticeable all through the war that we always appeared to come off lightly, even when other units in our vicinity suffered severely. The Battalion was withdrawn on 8 November 1917, after nearly four months of most difficult operations working under continuous shell fire. For practically the whole of this period we were living in bivouacs and temporary shacks improvised from any materials found lying about; and our camp was subjected to shelling and bombing day and night, but in spite of adverse conditions we received nothing but praise from those under whom we worked. Altogether, 50,000 yards (twenty-nine miles) of light railways were laid by the Battalion, which sustained some 200 casualties during the period. This figure of 50,000 yards takes no account, of course, of the innumerable repairs to breaks made in the lines by hostile fire. Many brave deeds were performed by volunteers, who never hesitated to go out and repair the damage under very heavy shell fire, and many of our brave men went out with the full knowledge that an almost certain and violent death awaited them.

It was while we were in this sector that the life-saving rum ration took on a new name. Lieutenant Colonel C.B. Charlesworth tells the story. 'I was talking to Joe Daly, our sanitary corporal, a real character, and was asking how he had slept the previous night, a nightmare of ceaseless bombing. "Oh, grand", he replied. "Well, you managed something I couldn't do", said I, to which Daly answered, "Yer want a good stiff tot o' rum, sir. Ah hed a double ration last neet; its grand, warms yer reight throo an maks yer feel champion, an yer goes straaght

Lieutenant Colonel C.B. Charlesworth was appointed Commanding Officer of 12th KOYLI on 29 September 1917.

off te sleep. Its t' finest stoof Ah've iver coom across. Elephant's blood Ah calls it!", and elephant's blood it remained to us forever afterwards'. For gallant conduct at various times during these four trying months the following decorations were awarded:

Major G.M. Stockings	-	Croix de Guerre (Belgian) and Mentioned in Dispatches.
Captain H.D. Gaunt	-	Military Cross.
Second Lieutenant W. Read	-	Military Cross.
CSM A. Hull	-	Croix de Guerre (Belgian)
CQMS H. Brittlebank	-	Croix de Guerre (Belgian)
CQMS G. Braper	-	Croix de Guerre (Belgian)
Corporal T. Mallender	-	Croix de Guerre (Belgian)
Corporal A. Jagger	-	Meritorious Service Medal

L.Corporal H. Ward	–	Military Medal
L. Corporal J.W. Garton	–	Military Medal
Private G.Hood	–	Meritorious Service Medal
Private K.E. Matherty	–	Meritorious Service Medal
Sergeant E. Bedford	–	Croix de Guerre (Belgian)
Private T. Wilson	–	Croix de Guerre (Belgian)

In the King's Birthday Honours List of June 1918, Captain F.H. White was awarded the Military Cross for most excellent work as Corps Tramway Traffic Officer since the summer of 1917.

Captain W. Baird and Lieutenant G. Walker were Mentioned in Dispatches for consistent good work and devotion to duty on many occasions.

The following awards were also made in the King's Birthday Honours List of June 1918, and were all conferred in recognition of gallant conduct during the work on the light railways in Flanders:-

Captain W. Cooper	–	Bar to Military Cross*
CSM Featherstone	–	DCM
CSM Parker	–	DCM
Sergeant E.J. Saynor	–	Meritorious Service Medal.
Private S. Holmes	–	DCM
Private F. Dawson	–	Military Medal.
Private W. Harrop	–	Mentioned in Dispatches
Private Spink	–	Mentioned in Dispatches

Some idea of the deadly character of this death-stricken salient during the period of our stay there can be obtained from the statement below, which was given to the House of Commons after the war had ended:

The total casualties suffered by the British, Canadian, Australian and New Zealand armies in the Ypres salient during the Passchendaele operations, which began on 31 July 1917 and ended on 6 November (the day the village of Passchendaele and the Passchendaele Ridge were captured) were 258,837, made up as follow:

---

* Captain Cooper's MC was gained during the operations between 11 and 13 April 1918.

	Officers	Other Ranks
British	10,795	207,838
Australian & New Zealand	1,289	26,502
Canadian	496	11,917
	12,580	246,257

[It is impossible to find the exact number of casualties sustained by both sides during the Third battle of Ypres. Captain England's figures for the British and Empire troops given above are almost in line with a number of books written on this subject over the past half century; the modern assessment being 275,000 casualties of whom 70,000 were dead.]

Chapter 8

Back to France again – Trench work near Roclincourt – Reorganisation of the Battalion into three Companies – An amusing incident – Departure of Major General R. Wanless-O'Gowan – Great German Offensive of 1918 – Initial German successes – The Commanding Officer is wounded – Relief of Battalion – Training at Cambligneul – Messages of appreciation for the 31st Division

On 20 November we boarded buses for Watten, and from there marched two miles to Ganspette, a small village just south of the big forest of Éperlecques; here we came under the orders of the 50th Division. Hardly had we got nicely settled in our comfortable billets when we were ordered to proceed to Renescure, thirteen miles away by route march, passing on our way through St. Omer, the small Flanders town where Lord Roberts died on 14 November, 1914 while visiting the British Expeditionary Force. [Born in India in 1832, Lord Roberts had served in the Indian Army then the British Army from 1851–1904 fighting in most of the campaigns in India and Afghanistan during this period. He commanded the British Army during the Boer War and in 1901 became Commander-in-Chief of the British Army.]

The next day we were taken in buses from Renescure to Ham-en-Artois (fourteen miles), two miles north of Lillers, and on 30 November, by bus again, to Camblingeul, nine miles north-west of Arras, where we rejoined the 31st Division, which was very pleased, we felt sure, to see us back again. Here we enjoyed a much needed rest after four weary months in the Ypres Salient. In addition to the physical exhaustion brought about by the continuous toil of working parties and the mental strain of incessant bombing and shelling, the whole Battalion was suffering from the very depressing morale effects of living for so many weeks in muddy shelters and cubby-holes. There was a great deal of cleaning up of both men and their equipment and a very vigorous programme of musketry and general infantry training had to be carried out. We were therefore kept fully occupied until 20 December. On this day parties from A and D Companies departed for various camps in the neighbourhood of Roclincourt, while Battalion HQ moved to Écurie on 22 December, where it occupied a Nissen hut camp that had previously been erected by a party under Lieutenant Partridge.

The 31st Division was again holding almost the same sector of the line as it was when the Battalion left it on 1 July, 1916; but what a change in the conditions. We now found things very quiet on this front and one could even buy a Grand Marnier at a canteen in the front line! Advantage was taken of the quietness to strengthen the defences and an elaborate system of trenches was begun, consisting of seven lines of defence each very strongly wired. These defences proved to be well worth the labour expended on them when the German attack came later, in March 1918.

We started the New Year in the usual manner, the Battalion being distributed in little parties here and there all over the countryside, and engaged on trench maintenance, dugout construction, tramway laying, wiring, etc. D Company had the honour of a special mention in the War Diary having, during the week ended 12 January 1918, wired in double apron style no less than 1,950 yards of the 'Brown' line; they figured again later when they were recorded as having wired 1,500 yards in the week, and had only sixty men with which to do it. In the last week of the month parties of several hundred men were loaned to us from 92 and 93 Brigades for general maintenance work, the task having got beyond our powers. Under the War Diary entry for 31 January, is the significant entry, 'All shell hole groups reported provided with trip wires in front, red and white warning boards, notice boards, tapes and guide pickets; exit steps made in trench and directing boards fixed.' What awful visions of ghastly days and terrifying nights does the mention of shell hole groups bring to mind, what memories of Herculean efforts by ration-carrying parties! The 8 February 1918 was a date of some importance, for on that day 4 Guards Brigade joined the Division and, whether justified or not, we felt considerable pride in the fact that these distinguished troops were to fight side by side with us. [This was part of the February 1918, reorganisation of the BEF. This did not apply to the Australian, New Zealand and Canadian divisions.] British infantry brigades were reduced from four to three battalions and each battalion reduced from four to three companies. The government's Manpower Committee had recommended to the Cabinet that all infantry Brigades should be reduced, and Field Marshal Haig was forced to restructure his army at the very time he was expecting the Germans to launch a major attack.]

From the beginning of February up to 3 March all hands were employed on trench and general works. Near the end of February orders were received for the reorganisation of all pioneer battalions on a three company basis, instead of the four then existing. This was sad news, but after weighty consideration it fell to the lot of A Company to be disbanded as this company had been recruited from various districts, whereas the other companies had been recruited each from a particular district. A Company was therefore re-organised on 3 March into three platoons, one being posted to each of the other companies. The transport had to be reduced proportionately, and the surplus was handed over to 9th Battalion, Durham Light Infantry. Surplus equipment and stores went to our old friend the DADOS [Deputy Assistant Director Ordnance Supplies] 31st Division. In this connection, Captain N.L Bennett relates an amusing episode; we reproduce the incident in his own words. Speaking of the handing over of tools, he says:

'This meant that we had to hand in to DADOS one quarter of all tools we were supposed to have according to Mobilisation Tables. As anybody who was in a pioneer battalion knows, the eight wagons of tools we took overseas were soon found to be particularly useless for modern warfare, and consequently they were gradually scrapped and other tools that were really needed were collected. The result was that we had not the tools to hand in; for instance, we had to hand in about 250 shovels of a particular type. We possessed not a single one, though we had plenty of shovels of a type that the men could use. I was Acting Adjutant at the time, and the Quartermaster (QM) came to me in distress (imagine ANY Quartermaster in distress, and particularly ours!). As we dare not admit the terrible truth to Divisional HQ, I applied to our good friends at the RE dump to see if they could help us. They, of course, could not supply all we needed, but they told me to send round a wagon and they would see what they could do. The wagon returned with all they had of the particular tools we required, ie. about a third of the number we had to hand in. I told the QM to take them round to DADOS and to say we could not spare the transport to bring any more that day, but that we would send the rest over the next day, hoping that in the meantime we might be able to collect some more from the Corps dump. The QM accordingly took them round to DADOS and got a receipt for eighty shovels, etc. With his ears well open, as usual, the QM heard the DADOS tell his staff sergeant to take the tools to the RE dump. The next morning our brainy QM drew the same tools from the RE dump, handed them over to DADOS again and got a receipt. This was repeated the third day, and thus it came about that we handed in the requisite number of tools.'

In the early days of March the Division was taken out of the line and moved into the Villers Châtel area, the Battalion going into billets at Camblingneul, C Company excepted, as they went on detachment for work on dugouts at Corps Headquarters in Écoivres, B Company relieving them on 15 March. Having completed the job, they rejoined the Battalion on the 19th day of the same month. On 20 March, amidst general regret throughout the Division, our Divisional Commander, Major-General R. Wanless-O'Gowan, CB, CMG, left us. He was succeeded by Major General R.J. Bridgford, CB, CMG, DSO, who very quickly found a warm spot in everyone's heart. In the meantime the rest of the Battalion began a period of strenuous training. This was not unconnected with the fact, plain to the British high command, that the general military situation towards the end of 1917 seemed to offer the Germans a possibility of conducting the war in the western theatre by means of an attack.

Ludendorff [General Erich Luddendorff – First Quartermaster-General of the German General Staff] says in his Memoirs of the War,

Throughout the latter half of 1917 I had strained every nerve to bring about the results that had now been attained, sparing myself no more than I spared others. The western front had held, the Italian army was defeated, and the Austro-Hungarian armies in Italy were inspired with new courage. The Macedonian front was holding out. In the east the armistice negotiations were finished, and the way to peace lay open to the diplomats. Negotiations at Brest Litovsk were to begin about Christmas. There was a prospect of our winning the war. Only in Asia Minor had there been any hitch, but the great events in Europe had pushed them into the background.

Under the influence of this hopeful outlook, the German Supreme Command decided in favour of a decisive battle in the western theatre of war in the spring of 1918 and all the plans for the great general attack were completed by the beginning of February 1918. The German strategic aim was the separation of the French and British Armies about Amiens, and with this in view the southern sector of the British Front was to be attacked first, as these troops were exhausted by the 1917 fighting, and it was considered desirable on general grounds to beat them first. When the British army was well rolled up and tucked away nicely between the Germans and the sea, then the French were to be chastised in the same way.

For a long time, indeed previous to March 1918, it had been obvious to the British high command that division after division of German troops, and battery upon battery of artillery had been rolling up from Italy and the Russian fronts until, according to figures given by Lieutenant Colonel W. Muller-Lophnitz, sixty-two divisions and 1,706 batteries were made available for the main attack, and Sir Douglas Haig, the British C-in-C, must have spent an anxious time awaiting the blow that he knew must be delivered within a short time. The German offensive of March–April 1918 was really composed of seven separate attacks, each with a distinctive code name, and each remarkably well prepared. Matters were so arranged that, in the event of any one of these attacks failing or being abandoned, unwanted men and material could be expeditiously switched over to any of the attacks which did show signs of yielding results. [Sometimes the overall plan is referred to as the 'Kaiserschlacht' or 'The Emperor Battle' and was planned to take place over the period 21 March – 15 July 1918.] The German code name for the operation was 'Michael' and the attack was to be made by the Seventeenth,

Second and Eighteenth Armies along a front some sixty miles wide. The individual attack (code name 'Mars') that concerns us most was along both sides of the Scarpe river and was made by the German Seventeenth Army, with its centre of gravity directed toward St. Pol. [Captain England only relates the events that occurred on the front defended by the 31st Division, one of nine, General Headquarters reserve divisions – the 8th, 31st and 41st that arrived at the front on the second day of the main attack. Operation Mars was planned as a strike in the area around Arras and was scheduled to take place some days after the main offensive had begun. However, despite the initial success of the Germans on this front, by the end of the first day they were loosing momentum. Ludendorff quickly closed down the Mars operation to concentrate on the success by his forces moving towards Amiens. Here, the German Eighteenth Army, attacking on a front of twenty miles, succeeded in crushing the British Fifth Army which brought about a general retreat that was only stopped when a few miles from the city of Amiens.]

Great forces of aircraft were concentrated on the fronts selected for the attacks and at the price of great sacrifices they succeeded by weight of numbers in preventing our aircraft observing any of their preparations for the forthcoming attack. All this was, of course, unknown to us as individuals, and our training at Cambligneul continued more or less peacefully until 21 March, when from our snug billets we had the first intimation of anything being amiss – a persistent and dull roaring of guns in the distance. As a matter of fact we had reached the final stages of the Divisional sports and boxing competitions, and a boxing match was actually in full swing when Brigadier General E.P. Lambert, CB, CMG, the Divisional artillery general, known throughout the Division as 'Stuffy Lambert', strolled into the arena and, in his driest manner announced, 'Gentlemen, the b....y Boche has pinched Bullecourt.'

On 21 March, at 9.40 am, the German infantry dashed forward to the assault, preceded by a creeping barrage of extraordinary intensity. As a result of this, our peaceful sleep was rudely shattered at 11 pm that night by an urgent message ordering the Battalion to be ready to leave by bus at three o'clock the following morning on the main road between Tincques and Tincquette, that is to say about half-way between Savy and St. Pol. We did eventually board our vehicles at 10 am on the appointed day and were taken to Bellacourt, a small village some few miles north-west of Bapaume, which we reached at six in the evening. The GOC 4 Guards Brigade, being the senior brigadier, sent for all commanding officers and, said Lieutenant Colonel C.B. Charlesworth, 'after showing us several telegrams all about breakthroughs by the Boche, announced quietly, "Gentlemen, I'm afraid we must fight tonight." We all looked down our noses and speedily rejoined our battalions.' Hardly had we completed our disembarkation when orders arrived to the effect that we were to proceed to Boisleux au Mont, nearly half-way between Arras and Bapaume, where we attached ourselves to various infantry units: B Company (Captain V. Mossop) to 11th Battalion East Yorkshire Regiment, C Company (Captain W.H. Roberts) to 11th Battalion East Lancashire Regiment, and D Company (Lieutenant J.N. Blenkin) to 10th Battalion East Yorkshire Regiment. Thus arranged, we marched on to the Army Line east of Hamelincourt, but had no time to begin any work there, for at 9am, 23 March, we were ordered to concentrate all companies at Moyenville, about two miles due west.

Information as to the actual situation was very scanty and most contradictory. It may strike the reader that this rapid succession of orders and our consequent dashes from place to place suggests a state of indecision amongst our immediate superiors; and indeed it was so. The German onrush had been so rapid and overwhelming that the British line was rolled back in great disorder, and it is no exaggeration to say that something approaching chaos prevailed. At Moyenville, the enemy having already reached Mory, about three miles to the south-east, we hung about for two hours awaiting orders from the Corps Chief Engineer, who apparently had a pressing engagement elsewhere, as he never turned up. The CRE 31st Division therefore, gave instructions for five supporting points to be constructed during the night, and for trenching work to be done on the 'Yellow Line'. Battalion HQ was temporarily established in Moyenville village, C Company constructed the strong points whilst B and D Companies connected up points in the Yellow Line. We had not worked long at these jobs when the whole Battalion was ordered to dig yet another line, known as the Green Line. It should be explained that for ease of reference the various defensive lines behind the front were always called the Red, Green and Yellow line, etc, the Red Line being the one nearest to the enemy. The next day, 24 March, at 5 pm, further shocks were administered to our already overwrought systems by the arrival of an order to the effect that, as the enemy was about to attack Gommiecourt, a small hamlet two miles away on our right flank (not to be confused with Gommecourt in the Department of the Somme), it would be highly desirable, and in fact necessary, for us to dig, fortify, and defend the eastern verge of Courcelles-le-Comte, a village one and a quarter miles to the north-west of Gommiecourt. The work was put in hand and by dawn of 25 March we had constructed a good defensive position and here, for a little time, we awaited events and further instructions. These, when they arrived, ordered the Battalion to take up a position immediately covering the Albert–Arras main railway line. We had to form up in the main street of Moyenville under heavy fire and while doing this Captain W.H. Roberts, Lieutenants H.B. Skevington and T.K. Cooper, together with several men of C Company, were wounded and three men killed. This delayed matters somewhat, but at last we moved off by companies. Things were rendered rather more unpleasant for us by our own artillery shooting short and plastering us and the countryside with the products of Britain's munitions factories.

On the night of 25/26 March, we had orders to withdraw to Douchy-lès-Ayette, a mile and a half to the rear, and at noon the next day (26 March) we received warning orders to be prepared to come into action, as the opposition was approaching rapidly from the south; but at 7.30 pm, as the result of late orders, we withdrew to Monchy-au-Bois, where a short night's rest was obtained in an old hut camp. Whilst reconnoitring, in company with the Divisional CBE (Commander Brigade Engineers) near Douchy on 26 March, our Commanding Officer, Lieutenant Colonel C.B. Charlesworth, was struck by a fragment of a German 5.9 inch shell; having narrowly escaped from total annihilation he managed to reach the Battalion. Nevertheless, on the same day we marched to Adinfer with the intention of digging a line east of the village, but on arrival at the destination were switched off this idea by 92 Brigade and instead we dug a line of posts in the vicinity of Quesnoy Farm. Touch was made on the right with 4th Grenadier Guards, and on the left with a trench mortar battery of 92 Brigade.

Early in the morning of 27 March we vacated the line of posts we had dug so arduously and shifted right in order to establish another line from Quesnoy Farm to Essarts. This line we dug and occupied at 6 am, the Grenadiers now being on our left and 42nd Division on our right. Things were not by any means quiet, but we sustained no casualties beyond Captain E. Forbes, RAMC, our esteemed medical officer, and Lieutenant L.F. Phillips, both of whom were wounded but remained on duty. At Essarts we were almost back once more to our old loves, Hébuterne and Serre; Gommecourt was only 1¾ miles in the rear and Hébuterne 2½ miles. As a result of his wound sustained on 26 March at Douchy, Lieutenant Colonel C.B. Charlesworth was unfortunately evacuated to hospital at noon on 28 March, and Captain G.S. Leach took over the command; Lieutenant L.F. Phillips was commanding B Company, Lieutenant J.K. Partridge was commanding C Company, and Lieutenant T.E. Oxley had D Company.

The Battalion now extended its front about 600 yards north-east of Quesnoy Farm and spent the night 28/29 March in improving trenches and dodging heavy shells. By daybreak the Huns had penetrated into the eastern part of Ayette and things generally were looking serious, as there seemed to be no stopping the German advance. The 3rd Battalion, Coldstream Guards held a line to our right along the Bucquoy road, with two companies of the Grenadier Guards in support. In order to free the Grenadiers for front line duty, 12th KOYLI took their place in support of the Coldstreams and during the night of 29 March we moved to the sunken road south-east of Douchy-lès-Ayette. The Battalion, being under the tactical command of the GOC 94 Infantry Brigade, had six platoons of B and D Companies, under Captain V. Mossop and Lieutenant T.E. Oxley, occupying some old German gunpits in front of the road, and were prepared to counter-attack if the Guards had been pushed back, while the remainder of the Battalion spent a most uncomfortable time in the sunken road itself. During the operations Second Lieutenant Lobel, MM, and seven ORs were wounded and one OR was killed. The situation underwent no change and on 31 March, at midnight, 16th Highland Light Infantry, 32nd Division, relieved the Battalion and we withdrew to Pommier, which was a nice wee village, very little damaged, though it was dark and dismal when we got there at five o'clock in the morning. We rested there a little, left at noon and went to

Ivergny, fourteen miles away, where we arrived at 5 pm and went into billets. Our strength on this evening was twenty-eight officers and 760 ORs.

Buses arrived the next morning and whirled us away once more to Cambligneul, Major G.M. Stockings rejoined us there after completing a course at Aldershot and took over the command from Captain G.S. Leach. From 3 to 9 April we had a happy time re-fitting and generally cleaning ourselves up. We also did much musketry training, which was a good thing, as it came in very useful within a week. Thus ended, as far as we were concerned, the first phase of the great German offensive of 1918. The following messages of appreciation of the services rendered by the 31st Division in connection with the operations were received:

From the Army Commander, 5th April, 1918.

> The GOC Third Army wishes to express to this Division on their leaving his command his appreciation of their conduct in the battles near Arras. By their gallantry and determination they helped to break up the most overwhelming attacks we have been subjected to during this war, and have borne a very noble share in preventing the enemy obtaining a decisive victory.

From the Corps Commander, 2nd April, 1918.

> The VI Corps Commander wishes to convey to all ranks of the 31st Division, on their leaving his Corps, his appreciation of the work done by them whilst under his command. The portion of the Corps front held by this Division was a very important one; its present satisfactory situation was due to the tenacity with which this front was held. The Divisional Commander wishes to join in this expression of satisfaction, and also to thank Brigade Staffs for their hard work.

From the Divisional Commander 25th March, 1918).

> The Corps Commander has expressed his high appreciation of the work done by the 31st Division. The GOC desires to associate himself

with this, and to convey his congratulations to the whole Division, and more especially, perhaps, to the 31st and 34th Divisional Artillery, the 4 Guards Brigade, the 92 Brigade, and the 31st Battalion Machine Gun Corps, on whom the greater part of the enemy attacks fell.

The following decorations were awarded for gallantry in connection with these operations:–

Captain G.S. Leach:	Military Cross.
Captain E. Forbes:	Military Cross.
Sergeant E. Ellis:	Military Medal.

The Battalion, with its usual good luck, came out of this action with the following casualties:–

Officers	six wounded
Other ranks	five killed, twenty-four wounded

In order to appreciate fully exactly what the BEF had accomplished it is necessary to consider the general situation at the end of March 1918. First of all it must be clearly understood that from the outset the fundamental idea of the German 'Michael' operation had been that of beating the British, and the British only. This achieved, the separation of the British and the French armies was merely a matter of time. The following summary is taken from an account of the battle by Lieutenant Colonel Wolfgang Foerster, late Chief of the General Staff, XI German Army Corps.

To this end the whole of the Seventeenth and Second German Armies were to fling themselves with all their might on the thin British line between the Somme river and Arras; up to midnight on 25 March the course of the battle justified the expectation of achieving its ambitious aim.

Everything depended on the south wing of the Seventeenth Army, which rested on the river at a point of support which was far too valuable to be lightly given up. The advance of this wing was, however, held up

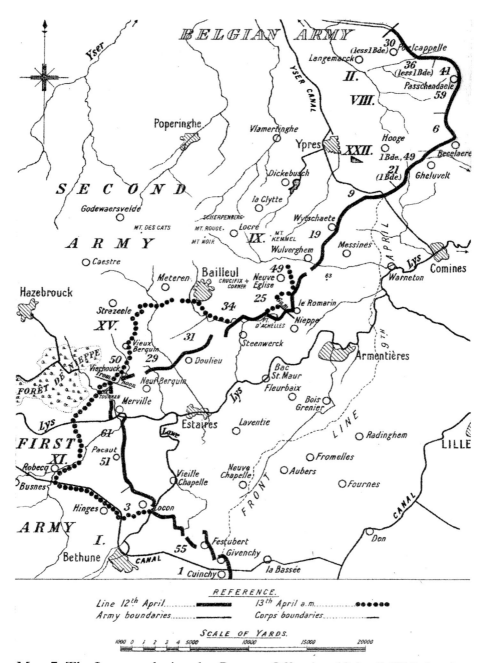

Map 7. The Lys area during the German Offensive, 12 April 1918 showing the 31st Division's position south of Bailleul.

by the heroic and unexpected stand of the British troops about the line of the Ancre.

But even then, all was not lost: a strong advance by the right wing of the Second Army across the river at Albert promised to be of great assistance, but the British defence was too stubborn. The Seventeenth Army between Arras and Albert could make no progress at all, and any further advance of the Second Army on its left would leave it with a flank in the air.

At this point, therefore, the operation against the British was finally abandoned on 30 March. In other words, we had administered a very severe check to Ludendorff's plan of separating the French and the British armies. It was nearly a fortnight before the Germans were able to mount a further attack on the Lys front; and the delay proved fatal to the whole scheme. Nevertheless, all was not *couleur de rose* on our side by any means. The enemy had not achieved full operative success, but they had dealt the British a heavy blow and crippled their fighting power for a long time to come. More than forty British divisions were seriously affected and also about twenty divisions of the French army had been drawn in to the fighting.

Chapter 9

Second phase of German Offensive – Hasty move to Vieux Berquin – Battle of La Couronne – Unfortunate predicament of the Transport Section – Gas shelling in Nieppe Forest – An encounter with a spy – Le Breard – Work in Flêtre and Caestre – Shelled out of Les Cinq Rues – Battalion sports at Staple – Influenza epidemic – A big wiring job – B Company lose their Headquarters – Training at L'Hofland – Experiences of prisoners of war – Move to the Meteren sector

It has previously been pointed out that the German offensive comprised several distinct attacks which were so designed that when one showed signs of failing another was launched to regain the momentum. Finding British resistance in the Artois region around Arras much more formidable than they had anticipated, the Germans broke off the battle on 30 March and decided immediately to put their 'Georgette' scheme into operation with a view to forcing a decision. It was planned to break through the British-Portuguese front in the direction of Hazebrouck and St. Omer then, continue the operation through St. Omer and Béthune and as far to the south as possible. For success it was essential to spring a complete surprise on the British. Preparations therefore had to be made in haste, and the German Sixth Army, under von Quast, fixed upon 9 April as the date for their attack. On that day, at 4.15 am, the German artillery bombarded our lines and back areas with enormous quantities of gas shells and succeeded in poisoning the ground for miles behind our front. At 8.45 am, the German infantry advanced to the assault and encountered only slight resistance, though they found the ground mist, which had favoured their assault, slowed down the pace of their advance. The Portuguese divisions in the Neuve Chapelle sector

Private George Barber Wood, (seated second row on the far left, soldier with pipe on page 5) was an original member of 12th KOYLI at Farnley Park.

were as good as annihilated and the Germans reached a line approximately running Sailly-Laventie-Richebourg L'Avoue-Festubert-Givenchy by the evening of 10 April.

During the first few days of April the Division had received large reinforcements comprised almost entirely of 18-year-old lads. Although only mere boys they were yet full of the optimism and excitement of youth, but almost untrained and quite unaware of the hardships of warfare. We received our quota and distributed our new acquisitions throughout the Battalion. They were destined to experience a very trying ordeal within a few days of their arrival.

On 10 April the Division was ordered to be in readiness to move at a moment's notice to the La Bassée-Laventie sector (XI Corps front), but at the eleventh hour these orders were changed and the Estaires-Bailleul sector (XV Corps front) was substituted. We knew what these orders meant, but we little realised that within a day or so we were destined to be handled very roughly indeed, worse, much worse than anything we had experienced up to now. The Battalion boarded buses at Vandalette, near Tincques, between Aubigny and St. Pol, at 4.30 pm that day and was transported as quickly as possible to Vieux Berquin, which was reached at 5.45 am the following day, a most uncomfortable hour of the day to arrive anywhere, but infinitely more so on this damp and miserable occasion. (See Map 8.) The transport column moved to Borre, where the Battalion details were, and parked with most of the other transport of the 31st Division. We then marched a mile or so to Merris and there installed ourselves in some bivouacs. By this time the enemy, who was showing great determination to get to the coast, had reached a line running Lestrem-Estaires-Pont Mortier. He fought very well and skilfully and appeared to have every chance of reaching his first strategic objective, Hazebrouck, a most important railway centre. Speaking generally, the outlook was pretty serious. [Hazebrouck had direct rail links with the Channel ports of Dunkerque, Calais and Boulogne, and most of the BEF's supplies for the northern section of the frontline from Arras to Ypres passed through this town.]

Such was the situation when, on the evening of 11 April, the Battalion received orders to take up a position astride the Estaires-Caestre road, covering the cross roads before La Couronne. This position was taken up by 9.30 pm, without opposition from the enemy.

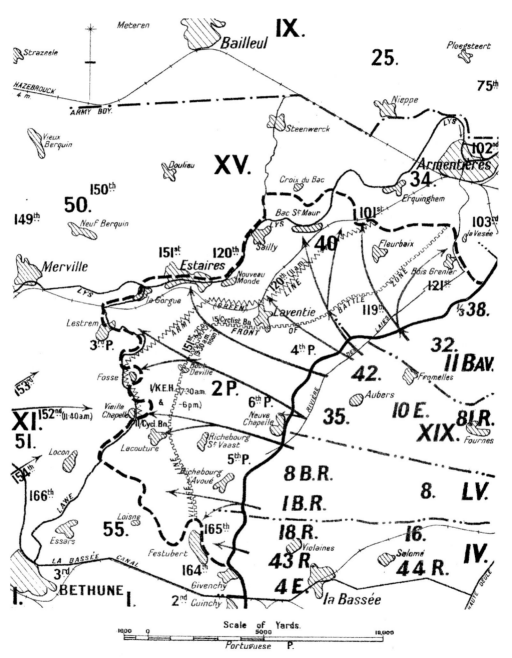

Map 8. The Battle of the River Lys, 9 April 1918. This battle was a smaller version of the German Michael Offensive in March 1918.

[The following Order of the Day, issued by Sir Douglas Haig, is not mentioned in the War Diary of 12th KOYLI. Neither Lieutenant Colonel Stockings nor Captain England make reference to it and there is a strong possibility that 12th KOYLI and most of the troops who fought alongside them on that day knew nothing of its existence but their instincts and training meant they fought in exactly the way their Commander-in-Chief had called for. Part of the order is reproduced here.]

Field Marshal Sir Douglas Haig's Special Order of the Day, 11 April 1918.
There is no other course open to us but to fight it out. Every position must be held to the last man: there must be no retirement. With our back to the wall and believing in the justice of our cause each one of us must fight on to the end. The safety of our homes and the freedom of mankind alike depend upon the conduct of each one of us at this critical moment.

The Official History of the Great War – Military Operations France and Belgium 1918, March –April, describes the position on 13 April as follows:

The sector directly covering Hazebrouck between Bourre and Merris (south-east of Strazeele) was held by the left wing of the 95 Brigade (5th Division); 4 Guards Bde (31st Divn); survivors of the 86 and 87 Bdes (29th Division), holding less than a thousand yards; and the 92 Bde (with details of the 92 and 93 Bdes attached as composite battalions) of the 31st Division.

From this it can be seen that the force being gathered to oppose the Germans was indeed a mixed one comprising anyone who could stand and fire a weapon. (See Map 9.) The following account of the action was written by Major (now Lieutenant Colonel) G.M. Stockings DSO, who was in command.

On the evening of the 11 [April], 12th KOYLI, with a strength of 529 commanded by Major G.M. Stockings, received orders from the 92 Brigade to take up a position astride the Estaires – Caestre road and

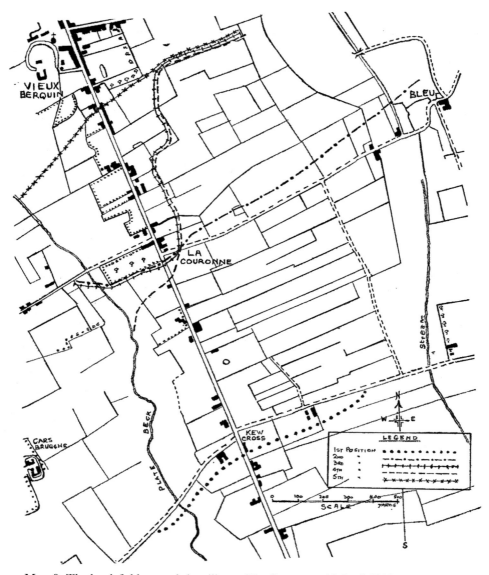

Map 9. The battlefield around the village of La Couronne, 13 April 1918. It was here that 12th KOYLI lost 13 officers and 275 men killed in action.

covering the cross roads in front of La Couronne. The enemy was reported to be advancing from the south and to have already reached that point. Two sections of the 31st Machine Gun Battalion were detailed to assist. The orders were to get into touch with troops on the flanks, especially with 92 Brigade on the left.

The positions indicated were occupied without opposition. B Coy, on the right under Captain V. Mossop, D Coy, on the left under Lieutenant J. Noel Blenkin, with C Coy, under Captain F.H. White, in reserve at La Couronne. A Field Coy of the 31st Divisional Royal Engineers had been ordered to assist, but did not arrive, having been employed elsewhere.

In spite of the efforts of patrols, who went much further than the positions indicated as being occupied by the 92 Brigade, the companies failed to get into touch with troops on either flank. Early in the morning of the 12, 4 Guards Brigade arrived, pushed forward on our right and attacked the enemy. Unfortunately for the 12th KOYLI, by a misunderstanding a large proportion of our shovels were handed over to them, so that henceforth throughout the action the majority of the men had only their entrenching tools left to them for digging purposes. The Guards also took forward with them the machine guns. On the arrival of the 4 Guards Brigade the 12th KOYLI came entirely under their orders for tactical purposes.

Towards noon orders were received from Brigade to take up a defensive position at the cross roads of La Couronne itself; the left was to extend as far as the hamlet of Bleu in the hope that touch could be gained with 92 Brigade, but in the event of failure to do so to refuse the

Lieutenant Colonel G.M. Stockings was in temporary command of 12th KOYLI from 28 March–10 October 1918. He commanded the Battalion during the fierce German attack in April 1918.

left flank and fall back still holding the cross roads of La Couronne, but covering the village of Vieux Berquin with a line facing east and southeast. The company still remaining forward of the cross roads was slightly withdrawn and the new dispositions placed B Coy on the right covering Verte Rue for about 400 yards west of La Couronne, D Coy from La Couronne eastwards for 500 yards, and C Coy on D Coy's left flank to Bleu. In conjunction with a party of Royal Engineers of the 50th Division and details of the Northumberland Fusiliers of the same division, a hastily constructed line was formed. Towards afternoon elements of the 29th Division, who were on the left front, began to fall back and came into alignment with the 12th KOYLI, thus filling the gap between them and the 92 Brigade.

About 3 pm, the enemy machine gun fire became heavy, with a considerable amount of shelling. Shortly afterwards, away on the left flank, troops could be seen falling back on the Vieux Berquin-Oultersteene Road, a retrograde movement which was presently taken up by the 29th Division. Therefore, in accordance with orders the left flank of the Battalion was refused and, pivoting on La Couronne, covered the village. The left was then facing east-south-east with the right in the same position as previous to the attack, La Couronne forming an elbow in the line. Touch was then gained with some of the South Wales Borderers on the left and the Grenadier Guards on the right. Thanks to the able leadership of the officers the somewhat difficult manoeuvre of changing the left flank from facing south to east under heavy fire was carried out in perfect order and with little loss. The fighting died down by about 7 pm; unfortunately Lieutenant Blenkin was at this time wounded by a bullet in the leg and had to retire, command of D Coy being passed on to Second Lieutenant Bingham; otherwise the loss had been slight. The night of 12 April was passed in the position described above, the men digging in as well as possible. A reinforcement of fifty men, under Second Lieutenant Wilson, arrived.

The morning of 13 April opened with a thick mist. About 8.30 am the enemy machine gun fire became very heavy and an attack began to develop. Four of these were beaten off, C Coy, under Captain F.H. White, causing the enemy particularly heavy casualties. The attacks seemed to be chiefly directed against La Couronne. At this time Second Lieutenant Bingham was killed and Second Lieutenants Palmer, Brierley, Atkinson and Clark wounded. The machine gun fire was intense, with a good deal of sniping by both sides. At 10 am Captain White reported that the enemy had succeeded in massing about 200 men in the lines we had made and evacuated on the previous day. The enemy then brought trench mortars to bear on the positions held by B Coy about the La Couronne cross roads, and after suffering heavy casualties this company was compelled to evacuate its position; this occurred about 11.30 am, B Coy then retired in good order to a line approximately 400 yards to the north-west. D Coy, which was now under the command of Second Lieutenant Meek, also had to fall back to conform with the new line, C Coy remaining in the position it had held since the previous night.

The Battalion's right flank now rested on the Plate Beck, a stream of considerable size, astride the main road facing south-east, and about 400 yards north-west of La Couronne. Touch had been lost with the Grenadier Guards on the right, but on the left it was maintained with the 1st Lancashire Fusiliers (29th Division.). The men dug in rapidly with their entrenching tools and again put up an obstinate resistance to the advance of the enemy. At this time it was evident that the enemy had succeeded in bringing up more guns as the shelling increased. A patrol under Sergeant Hirst of B Coy succeeded under heavy fire in getting through to the Irish Guards, from whom useful information was obtained as to the position on the right flank. Acting on this information, the Adjutant (Captain W. Cooper) gallantly endeavoured under very heavy fire to improve the disposition on the right and whilst so doing was seriously wounded.

About 2 pm, the enemy, having worked down the Verte Rue and along the houses and hedges about the main road between Vieux Berquin and La Couronne, enfiladed with machine gun fire the new line taken up by B Coy and also succeeded in working round C Coy's right flank; this broke the line and the Battalion was faced with the prospect of annihilation, capture, or retirement. The remnants fell back in good order and rallied at La Becque Farm, but cross machine gun fire made the position untenable. They then retired on to the line which the Australian 1st Division had had time to construct in the rear and assisted in holding it through the night of 13 April till withdrawn on the following morning. The few officers left had shown great gallantry and self sacrifice during the difficult task of withdrawing their men. Captains Mossop and White were both wounded, the latter very badly.

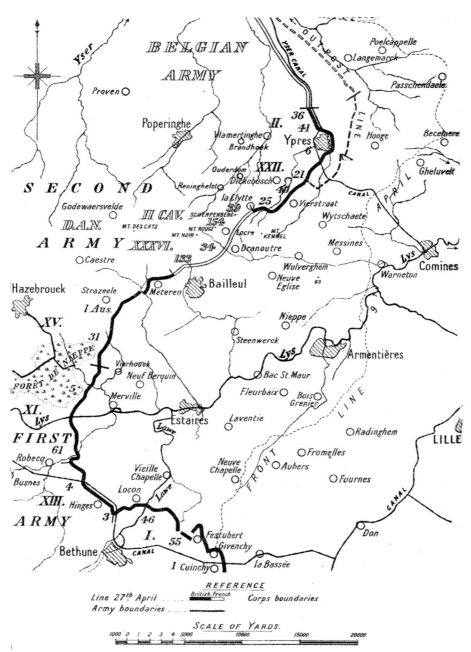

Map 10. This map shows how close the Germans came to capturing Hazebrouk by 27 April 1918

In addition to being outnumbered, 12th KOYLI had no artillery support against the enemy, who fought with great determination and skill. The stubborn defence had important results; it inflicted heavy losses on the enemy, and it protected the left flank of 4 Guards Brigade, thus enabling it to put up a longer and more punishing defence than it otherwise would have done, which gave 1st Australian Division time to detrain, make their dispositions and dig in. Furthermore, the enemy's threatened breakthrough was completely stopped on this portion of the front (See Map 10).

The Battalion went into action with a total of nineteen officers and 510 ORs. Of these, thriteen officers and 275 ORs were killed, wounded or taken prisoner. All three company commanders and the Adjutant were wounded.

The rebuilding of La Couronne taking place in 1922. The name does not appear on modern road maps but there are still some houses on either side of the Vieux Bequin – Neuf Bequin road where the action took place.

[The Official History, Military Operations France and Belgium, 1918, Vol II, published in 1937, some years after Captain England's history was written, records that 'A weak and tired Guards brigade, with a weak pioneer battalion attached, had made a glorious defence against four German regiments, each equivalent in infantry to a British brigade and, with the remainder of the 31st and 29th Divisions, had covered the detrainment of the 1st Australian Division, and saved Hazebrouck. To quote the words of Sir Douglas Haig's despatch: "The performance of all troops engaged in this most gallant stand, and especially that of the 4 Guards Brigade, on whose front of some 4,000 yards the heaviest attacks fell, is worthy of the highest praise. No more brilliant exploit has taken place since the opening of the enemy's offensive, though gallant actions have been without number."

Private William Davis, 12th KOYLI (see photograph on page 11) was killed in action during the intense fighting around La Couronne during the German Georgette offensive, 13 April 1918. His name is recorded on the Ploegsteert Memorial.

The most senior officer in the German Army made this observation on the result of the fighting during this period:

Field Marshal Paul von Hindenburg's account of the battle from 11 April onwards.

From now on progress became slower. It soon came to a stop on our left wing, while our attack in the direction of Hazebrouck was slowly becoming paralysed. On our centre we captured Balleul and set foot on the hills from the south. Wytschaete fell into our hands, but then this first blow was exhausted.]

The following are extracts from messages of congratulation received in connection with these operations:-

(a) From GOC First Army [General Sir Henry Horne] to GOC XV Corps [Lieutenant General Sir J. Du Cane) (13th April, 1918). 'I wish to express my appreciation of the great bravery and endurance with which all ranks have fought and held out during the last five days against overwhelming numbers. It has been necessary to call for great exertions, and more must still be asked for, but I am quite confident that at this critical period, when the existence of the British Army is at stake, all ranks of the First Army will do their very best.'

(b) From GOC, XV Corps to GOC, 31st Division. (Major General R.J. Bridgford) (13th April, 1918). The following received from the Army Commander. 'The Army Commander wishes to congratulate all the troops that have been engaged in the recent heavy fighting on their stubborn and determined resistance. He realises the severe test that they have been put to and the steadiness that they have displayed reflects the greatest credit on them. The Corps Commander wishes to add his thanks and congratulations.'

(c) From GOC, Second Army (General Sir Herbert Plumer) to GOC, XV Corps (17th April, 1918). 'The Army Commander wishes to place on record his appreciation of the gallant conduct of the troops under your command in the present fighting. It is worthy of all praise and he wishes all ranks to be informed.'

(d) From GOC, XV Corps, to GOC, 31st Division. (17th April, 1918). 'The Corps Commander wishes you to convey to the troops of your Division his appreciation of their courage and resolution during the period 12th to 14th April when opposed to greatly superior numbers. The fine stand on the 13th April by your Brigades when much depleted had an important bearing on the course of the operations.'

(e) From the Commander-in-Chief (Field Marshal Sir Douglas Haig), dated 24th April, 1918. 'The Corps Commander at a meeting of Brigadier Generals on 18th April expressed the Commander-in-Chief's congratulations on the fine work of the Division, especially on the 13th April, in saving a critical situation. He wished to thank the Division personally as he considered the work done really magnificent.'

(f) From the Commander-in-Chief to GOC, II Army (1st May, 1918). 'The magnificent performance of the 31st Division in holding up the enemy's advance at a critical stage of the Lys battle has already been publicly acknowledged. I wish to add my personal tribute to the fine fighting qualities displayed by this Division both on that occasion and also during the opening battle south of Arras. Please convey my thanks to the General Officer Commanding, and to all ranks of his command.'

(g) From the Commander-in-Chief's Dispatch, dated 23rd April, 1918. 'On April 13th the 31st Division was holding a front of some 9,000 yards east of Nieppe Forest. The Division was already greatly reduced in strength as a result of previous fighting and the enemy was still pressing his advance. The troops were informed that their line had to be held to the last to cover the detraining of reinforcements and all ranks responded with the most magnificent courage and devotion to the appeal made to them. Throughout a long day of incessant fighting they beat off a succession of determined attacks. In the evening the enemy made a last great effort and by sheer weight of numbers overran certain portions of our line, the defenders of which died fighting but would not give ground. Those of the enemy who had broken through at these points were, however, met and driven back beyond our lines by the reinforcing troops which by this time had completed their detrainment.'

And here is an extract from an article on the stand of the Guards' Brigade, which appeared in *The Times* newspaper of 2 May, 1918.

Close to the Guards, and earning the admiration of the Guards themselves, were some Yorkshire Light Infantry, a Pioneer Battalion, who held part of the line most determinedly and as well as the best infantry battalion could have done. The whole performance, indeed, seems to have been the most gallant possible. Our losses, as indicated, were severe, but there is no manner of question that the enemy's were infinitely heavier, and as an exhibition of stubborn, bull dog fighting it was magnificent.

The following decorations were awarded for gallantry during this action :—

Captain and Adjutant W. Cooper	- Military Cross
Captain V. Mossop	- Military Cross
Lieutenant J.N. Blenkin	- Military Cross
Lance Corporal W. Price	- Military Medal
Sergeant Knowles	- Military Medal
Sergeant H.B. Wade	- Military Medal
Lance Sergeant E. Parker	- Military Medal
Lance Corporal J. Price	- Military Medal
Private A.R. Mulligan	- Military Medal
Corporal F. Brown	- Bar to Military Medal
Private J. Bedford	- Military Medal
Private T.W. Saville	- Distinguished Conduct Medal

In Sir A. Conan Doyle's book, *The British Campaign in France and Flanders*, two flattering references to our Battalion are made. The first says: 'The readjustment of the line enabled the 4 Guards Brigade to link up with the 12th K.O. Yorks. L.I. pioneer battalion of their own division, which was holding the line at La Couronne and fought that day with the utmost tenacity and resolution. On the left flank of the Yorkshiremen, near Vieux Berquin, were the worn remains of the 29th Division.'

The second reference concerns the attaining of our celebrated nickname of 'Yorkshire Guards', which is referred to more fully later in this history; 'The 12th Yorkshire Light Infantry was also four separate times attacked but held to its appointed line. This gallant unit fairly earned the title of the "Yorkshire Guards" that day, for they were peers of their comrades ... .'

And finally let us read an extract taken from Field Marshal Sir Douglas Haig's Dispatch covering the period from 8 December, 1917, to 30 April, 1918, which appeared in the *London Gazette* on 21 October, 1918.

Next day (13th April, 1918) the enemy followed up his attacks with great vigour and the troops of the 29th and 31st Divisions, now greatly reduced in strength by the severe fighting already experienced and strung out over a front of nearly 10,000 yards east of the Forest of Nieppe, were once more tried to the utmost. Behind them the 1st Australian Division, under the command of Major-General Sir H.B. Walker, KCB, DSO, was in process of detraining and the troops were told that the line was to be held at all costs until the detrainment could be completed. During the morning, which was very foggy, several determined attacks in which a German armoured car came into action against the 4 Guards Brigade, on the southern portion of the lines, were repulsed with great loss to the enemy. After the failure of these assaults he brought up field guns to point blank range, and in the northern sector, with their aid gained everywhere except at Vieux Berquin, the enemy's advance was held up all day by desperate fighting in which our advanced posts displayed the greatest gallantry, maintaining their ground when entirely surrounded, men standing back to back in their trenches and shooting in front and in rear. In the afternoon the enemy made a further determined effort and, by sheer weight of numbers, forced his way through the gaps in our depleted line, the surviving garrisons of our posts fighting to the last where they stood with bullet and bayonet.

However, the heroic resistance of these troops had given the leading brigades of the 1st Australian Division time to reach and organise their appointed line east of the Forest of Nieppe. These now took up the fight and the way to Hazebrouck was definitely closed.

The performance of all the troops engaged in this most gallant stand, and especially that of the 4 Guards Brigade on whose front of some 4,000 yards the heaviest attacks fell, is worthy of the highest praise. No more brilliant exploit has taken place since the opening of the enemy's offensive, though gallant actions have been done without number.

The action of these troops, and indeed of all the divisions engaged in the fighting in the Lys valley, is the more noteworthy because, as already pointed out, practically the whole of them had been brought out of the Somme battlefield, where they had suffered severely and had been subjected to a great strain.

The papers at home were, of course, full of accounts, sketches, and photographs of the fighting, and *The Graphic* published a drawing of the heroic 4 Guards Brigade charging on to the main road in La Couronne. To this we were bound to take mild exception, for the sketch showed our own position during the action and it was actually 't'owd Twelfth' which was responsible for all the scrapping on the occasion depicted; the Guards were away on our right flank. A little incident which occurred after the fighting was over is worth recording. A batch of German prisoners was being interrogated and they were asked if they knew who was opposed to them. 'Oh, yes', they replied, 'the Grenadier Guards, the 3rd Coldstream Guards, the Irish Guards, but who are these Yorkshire Guards?' This was high praise indeed, and much more was received from the Guards themselves, who could desire no more worthy comrades than our lads, and had no hesitation in saying so.

As we have already related, the Battalion transport moved to Borre on 10 April where they arrived at 11 pm, at which hour it was, of course, quite dark. When they woke up in the morning, however, it was found to the general consternation that the camp was on the forward slope of a hill and in full view of the enemy! As soon as this awkward mistake was found out all the animals and vehicles were shifted with surprisingly little delay to a large farm about a mile north of Pradelles. Unfortunately, this apparent haven of rest was invaded at 5 pm by a battalion of 29th Division, who declared that the enemy was coming through Strazeele, only 1½ miles away, and that they were going to dig and man a line around the farm. Obviously, this was no place for so meek and mild a body of men as the Transport Section, and an intimation to Divisional HQ of their predicament resulted in the order that they had better move to Longue Croix, right behind Hazebrouck and this they did with great speed, arriving at 4 pm on 13 April. On 14 April, the Battalion was withdrawn from the line and marched into billets half a mile north of Borre as part of Corps Reserve.

Owing to our losses and the difficulty experienced in obtaining reinforcements, the Battalion was reorganised on 15 April into three companies of only two platoons each. Company commanders were: B Company, Major K.E, Aitken; C Company, Captain G.R. Atkinson; D Company, Captain W. Baird, with Captain N.L. Bennett as Adjutant. The next day, we were brigaded with 4 Guards Brigade and received orders to be prepared to man the Hazebrouck defences at an hour's notice. We heard on this day of the death of Captain F.H. White as a result of wounds sustained on 13 April near La Couronne. He was a most enthusiastic young officer and had commanded the Lewis gun detachment right from the beginning.

On 17 April we moved into billets and bivouacs near Le Tir Anglais in the Hazebrouck defences. Here we worked for two days improving the trenches generally and at 6.30 pm on the night of 19 April, the Brigade having relieved 7 Australian Infantry Brigade, the Battalion took over the right sector on the eastern verge of the Bois d' Aval, a portion of the big Forest of Nieppe. For this purpose we were again reorganised into two companies of three platoons each; B and D Companies each having a platoon of C Company attached. The transport established itself near Wallon Cappel. The Battalion held the left sector of the brigade front and all platoons were in the front line. The sector was fairly quiet but, on 21 and 22 April, the whole neighbourhood was subjected to a heavy gas shell bombardment; it was estimated in fact that some 3,000 gas shells were thrown into the wood in the first twenty-four hours! That is more than one every half-minute for a whole day. It may be convenient here to give a short explanation of the different kinds of poisonous gases of which we had experience and their uses.

It is well known that the Germans made the first use of gas when, on 22 April 1915, they discharged great quantities of chlorine on the Ypres front with great success from their point of view. The British followed suit at Loos in September of the same year, but there were serious difficulties in the way of its practical use, and cloud gas attacks were comparatively rare by the time we arrived on the scene. Our experience was confined to gas shells, of which prodigious quantities were used by all the combatants. The gases we used were phosgene (carbonyl chloride), a very dangerous gas because the effect is delayed and a victim was often unaware that he had been gassed and would drop dead quite suddenly as much as 48 hours after exposure to the gas; diphosgene, very similar to phosgene in its effects (trichlormethyl chloroformate); chloropicrin, attacking the respiratory system forming in the presence of water hydrochloric acid which destroyed the tissues. It had also a powerful lachrymatory effect, that is to say it affected the eyes to such an extent as to temporarily blind a person exposed to even so weak a concentration as one part in 1,000,000. Another very powerful lachrymator was bromine, which acted similarly to chlorine. Then we had diphenylchloroarsine (the celebrated

Blue Cross shell) which was a very fine powder and caused terrific headaches. This was later superseded by diphenylcyonarsine, similar in its effects but much more powerful. Lastly, the notorious mustard gas, alias Yperite, alias Yellow Cross (sym. dichlorodiethylsulphide). This invention of the devil penetrated the clothing and attacked all the mucous surfaces of the body, causing terrible burns and blisters. Moreover, it was of very high persistence and in suitable weather a spot shelled with this gas was poisoned for days afterwards. The most favourable atmospheric conditions for the use of gas shells are:- a) Little or no wind. b) Moist atmosphere. c) No sun. Therefore it will be readily understood that the night usually offered the best combination of conditions and we got our full share of poison whenever the enemy thought the conditions appropriate to use it. All three of the conditions given above were present in Nieppe Forest and we lived in a gaseous atmosphere for several days. In consequence, our gas casualties were very heavy indeed; seven officers, including Lieutenant Colonel G.M. Stockings, and about 150 other ranks being evacuated to hospital from this cause.

Lieutenant E. Simpson tells an interesting story of an incident which occurred during our tour of duty in the Bois d' Aval.

We had not had any sleep for two days and Bennett and I were lying down resting for a moment in a log hut. To our great surprise in came a major wearing a XV Corps armlet. We were very surprised to see him because it was 1 am and such visits were unusual. He said that he wanted to blue pencil on his map the exact position of our line and begged us not to disturb our CO, who was asleep. Bennett had a slight suspicion that all might not be well, and he went out to ask the Commander of the Irish Guards, with whom we were sharing a headquarters, whether we should give him the information. Colonel Alexander said "Yes, if he has a car." Bennett found the car, complete with chauffeur, and consequently came back to help him mark his map. In the meantime I had been chatting with him, and he certainly seemed absolutely all right. I remembered after, though, that he mopped his face frequently and said he was hot. There was perspiration there all right, but it was not heat that caused it! After marking his map, off he went. A few days after I got one of my friends on XV Corps Signals to find out if an officer from 'G' had been up the line at 1 am on the day in question. No staff officer, 'G' or otherwise, had been anywhere near our HQ on that day, and there can be no doubt that Bennett and I were twitted [made to look like twits] by a very clever spy. It was soon after this incident that exceedingly stringent orders were issued regarding spies.

The Battalion was relieved on the night of 22 April, and retired into support, taking over the front line again on 25 April which we held until the night of 27 April, when 29th Division relieved us. We went into camp near Hondeghem and the transport joined us there. The 31st Division was now in Corps Reserve and we, in common with the rest of the Division, were prepared to move at an hour's notice, Major D.E. Roberts replacing Lieutenant Colonel G.M. Stockings in command, with Captain G.S. Leach as second in command. Incidentally, it should be stated that the Battalion on its relief ceased to form part of 4 Guards Brigade. After a day's rest, and receiving a large number of reinforcements, the whole Battalion commenced work on the Corps Defence Line, just east of Hazebrouck. It should also be mentioned that the reinforcements enabled us to re-form into three companies of four platoons each, much to the satisfaction of company commanders and quartermaster sergeants.

From 2 to 8 May one company per day was off works for the purpose of training, and a considerable amount of musketry practice was put in. We heard a startling rumour on 8 May, to the effect that the Germans were about to attack on our front with sixty-one divisions and artillery to match, but much to our relief the expected onslaught did not take place. The Battalion relieved the 1st Battalion Australian Pioneers in the Meteren sector on 9 May, and for this purpose we moved to Le Brearde, between Hondeghem and Caestre, where the men encamped, some in tents and some in bivouacs, while most of the officers found accommodation in the half dozen or so cottages which comprised the hamlet. Night bombing was by this time rife, British and enemy machines droning across the sky the whole night long en route for choice targets such as Cassel, Hazebrouck and Armèntieres (the latter now in enemy hands) and so on. As a matter of fact, German aeroplanes during the war dropped about one million bombs altogether, and 700 of these were of the monster 1,000 kilogram type (about a ton). One poor Hun was in such a hurry to 'lay his eggs' that he did so at random in the fields around Le Brearde and administered a severe shock to Battalion Headquarters in doing so. Some French troops were holding the line round about Locre and whilst at Le Brearde we were greatly interested in watching them catch frogs in a pond close by. The method they used was: the fisherman, having procured a sapling about seven feet long, fixed a line of about the same length to one end. To the end of this line he tied a small morsel of meat and round the meat ran a couple of turns of ordinary darning wool. Thus armed he waded into the water and dangled the bait before a frog. In due course the frog made a dart for the meat and at the same instant the frog-fisher jerked his rod up in the air and up went the frog with it. The presence of the wool in some way or other prevented the frog letting go of the bait as quickly as he otherwise would have done. Meanwhile the fisherman's assistant had sighted the frog sailing through the air and had retrieved it. Then, he produced a pen-knife and with one stroke severed the head and forelegs from the body; with another skilful stroke he peeled the skin completely off the hind legs and dropped them into a handy bucket of clean water. The discarded head and forelegs walked on their own about the field for quite a long time. The flesh was quite white and when cooked in butter to a lovely pale brown was perfectly delicious, as we found by experiment. There were hundreds and hundreds of these frogs in all the ponds and ditches, and the noise they made during the night with their croaking was quite extraordinary and must be heard to be appreciated. It is a well authenticated fact that on this front the Germans found that the frogs interfered to such an extent with their sound ranging plant that eventually they had to abandon the use of their apparatus.

Battalion HQ was later shifted to Alum Farm, near Caestre; B Company, which was working on the defences of that village, encamped with HQ, C Company bivouacked in the Reserve Line near Le Roukloshille and worked on the Reserve Line, whilst D Company was billeted just outside Flêtre at St. Jean Farm and worked on the Flêtre defences. In the event of a hostile attack these companies were to form the nucleus garrisons of the defences. Details and the Quartermaster's Stores remained at Le Brearde, where a 25 yard rifle range was rigged up in an old heavy gun emplacement, and a platoon came down from the line every three or four days for rest and general training. Lieutenant Colonel G.M. Stockings returned from hospital on 14

May and took over from Major D.E. Roberts; he remained in temporary command of the Battalion, except for one or two very brief intervals, right up to 10 October, when Lieutenant Colonel C.B. Charlesworth rejoined.

With the capture of Meteren and Mount Kemmel by the Germans on 25–26 April, the Battle of the Lys, or as some call it the Battle of Armentières, came to an end, with the strategic honours on the side of the enemy, and our work in this sector was undertaken in anticipation of another attack by them as soon as they had consolidated their new positions and completed their arrangements for a new offensive. Generally speaking we had a fairly comfortable time for these fifteen days, though D Company suffered rather from gas and other shelling of Flêtre. On the night of 19 May, Lieutenant G.P. Morgan had a narrow escape from death when the house which he was converting into a strong point was struck by a shell and set on fire. He was severely wounded by the explosion and lay amidst the blazing debris, but Sergeant J.E. Munns, though himself badly wounded by the same shell, pluckily went to his rescue. For this very gallant act Sergeant Munns was awarded the Military Medal. Second Lieutenant T. Dann had been wounded by shell fire on the previous day, and the acute shortage of officers now became a serious problem. On 23 May the Battalion was relieved by 9th Battalion Seaforth Highlanders and moved into a tent camp in the railway triangle near Les Cinq Rues (XV Corps Area,), where we did some training, held kit inspections and received various reinforcements. This place was not a bit nice, but this was hardly surprising, since an important railway junction only eight miles from the front line is hardly likely to be as peaceful as a monastery garden with the result that we breakfasted on 5.9s, lunched on salvos from eight-inch howitzers and, when the shades of night had fallen, were rocked to sleep amidst the deafening crashes of giant aeroplane bombs. The extremely talkative lady at the farm house near D Company's mess will long be remembered by us and, we have no doubt, by a certain Australian transport unit also. This female, who had a very nimble tongue, was never tired of twitting the Aussies with the allegation that they had run away from a 'petit obus boche' [small German shell]. In reality, as several shells of hefty calibre had arrived in their camp at breakfast time one day, the Australians had merely shifted their animals to a safer spot. When dealing with 8 inch shells discretion is always the better part of valour. We could get no rest or peace in this area on account of the incessant shelling and bombing, so on 28 May we moved into a fresh area near Staple, each company being in a separate little camp of its own a couple of hundred yards from the others. This really was a quiet spot. From here companies proceeded to their work of cable laying, while one company was off daily for general training and musketry practice.

The 2 June was a red-letter day, for on that date the Battalion sports were held in a spacious meadow adjoining Battalion HQ. An official totalizer was set up and official bookies appointed by the Master of Ceremonies, Captain G.S. Leach, who was responsible for the general organisation of the proceedings and deserved the greatest credit for his very able management. Everything was done in proper style, the sprinters ran their 100 yards between the regulation posts and tapes, but we fear that no one did the distance in anything like 10.15 seconds. Every competitor managed to rig himself up in an athletic costume of some kind, though several of the fashions were rather bizarre. There was, for instance, the high jump expert, who turned up in a red and white football jersey, shorts of a very faded blue, and vivid yellow stockings. The runners were started by the simple expedient of firing a blank from a skeleton action [pistol] borrowed, much to his disgust, from Sergeant Bissett, the Armourer Sergeant. Then there was the sack race, when the competitors were so enthusiastic that they trod holes in their sacks and raced along unimpeded. The commencement of each event was signalled by the tolling of a large bell, obtained from some poor wrecked church we fancy, but one did not ask where such articles were actually obtained, and there was some slight confusion when it was found that two races had been started simultaneously from opposite sides of the course! A collision of the parties in the middle of the field was happily averted just in time, and the race re-started. The piece de resistance was, of course, the inter-company tug-of-war, which created terrific excitement and a certain private of B Company was observed to be 'making a book' of his own on the event. Unfortunately, no records of this epoch-making day were kept and we cannot remember the winners of the prizes, which ranged from jack-knives, chocolate bars and packets of cigarettes to small sums of money. Anyway, the whole affair was most enjoyable and was voted a huge success from every point of view, except that of the bookie – he lost heavily. As a result of this little venture the Canteen Fund benefited, we think, to the extent of very nearly £50.

An epidemic of influenza broke out on 10 June and raged for nearly a fortnight, an average of about ninety men per day being on the sick list, in addition to which seventy to eighty men were evacuated to hospital. About half the British Army was down with the disease at the time, and the German Army was understood to be in a similar plight. On 15 June, the Division was brought back to the forward areas as an enemy attack was anticipated. The Battalion was brigaded with 94 (Yeomanry) Infantry Brigade, which had joined the Division in place of 4 Guards Brigade and battle positions in the West Hazebrouck defences were reconnoitred. The expected enemy attack not having materialised, the Division went back to the rest area and companies returned to their camps at Staple.

The Division relieved 29th Division on 21 June in the Nieppe Forest sector and our battalion took over from 1st/2nd Battalion Monmouthshire Regiment (Pioneers). They had been billeted in cottages and tents around the cross roads at L'Hofland, barely a mile to the east of Hazebrouck. The houses were practically undamaged and we made ourselves comfortable. All companies went on works; B Company on a line at Petit Sec Bois, and C and D Companies in the forest itself (Bois d' Aval portion). On 24 June the three companies relieved the garrisons of three fortified points in the Hazebrouck scheme: B Company took over the Swartenbrouck line from a company of 13th York and Lancs Regiment and came under the orders of 8th Durham Light Infantry; C Company (now under the tactical command of 92 Brigade) garrisoned the La Motte defences in succession to 11th Battalion York and Lancs Regiment; while D Company replaced a company of 13th Battalion York and Lancs. Regiment in the Petit Sec Bois defences and took their orders from 15th Battalion West Yorkshire Regiment. There was no time to be idle and, in addition to improving and strengthening their respective defences, all the companies did wiring, hurdle and fascine making and tramway laying.

Battalion HQ, Quartermaster's stores and details remained at L'Hofland. On the railway line just at the back of their billets was a 15 inch gun, which was firing principally into Armentières, fifteen miles away as the crow flies, then a vast depot of German stores and munitions. When this beastly thing went off the concussion was dreadful and such a back draught was set up that windows were blown open and lamps and candles extinguished. However, they could only manage to fire once every fifteen minutes, which was something to be thankful for. The crew exhibited signs of jubilation one day and on enquiring the cause we were informed that thanks to good spotting by their attendant aeroplane they had registered three direct hits on the main German ammunition dump and had set the whole thing well alight.

An attack was delivered by the Division in conjunction with 5th Division on the right on the morning of 28 June, the front line being pushed forward about 500 yards. Owing to the nature of the ground a continuous line of trenches could not be dug and the new line was composed of posts. When night fell, the whole Battalion, having been temporarily relieved of its garrison duties, set to work to erect a continuous belt of wire in front of the line. The preparation for this work, which necessitated the use of great quantities of wiring material, needed very careful organisation and the employment of large infantry carrying parties. 92 Brigade delivered much of the material up to the line by means of a convoy of sixty mules. All the posts were successfully wired with one exception, which could not be completed owing to heavy enemy artillery and machine-gun fire. However, a platoon of D Company went out the next night and finished the job and altogether about 1,100 yards of entanglement were erected and only half a dozen men were wounded. All three companies (which were commanded as follows: B Company, Lieutenant J. Downs; C Company; Captain G.R. Atkinson; D Company, Captain W. Baird), were heartily congratulated by the commanding officers of the infantry battalions holding the posts, and in addition Captain Baird was awarded the Military Cross for his share in the proceedings. Lieutenant Colonel A.W. Rickman, DSO, commanding 93 Infantry Brigade, referring to this work, wrote, 'The work performed by these troops was of inestimable value to the operations and I cannot speak too highly of the way in which it was carried out.' Again, Lieutenant Colonel C.H. Gurney, commanding 11th Battalion East Yorkshire Regiment, wrote, 'The 12th KOYLI also did some excellent work in consolidating and wiring posts, B and C Companies under heavy fire, which made work extremely difficult. The officers and other ranks were an example to all.' Having completed their task, the companies returned to their former garrison posts as previously described.

As so much mention has been made of wiring it will perhaps be not inappropriate if a brief description of the operation is inserted here. In the first place it must not be imagined that it was a job which could be lightly undertaken. Nor was it a case of marching one hundred or so men on to the job and setting to work in a haphazard fashion. Lives and materials were too valuable to risk wastage. On the other hand the erection of an efficient screen of barbed wire was of immense importance, so important indeed that Major General Sir Neill Malcolm, KCB, DSO, in a work on Tactics, wrote: 'after three months of moving warfare the siege of Germany began. Once started, it lasted for four whole years, a phenomenon which was due to field fortifications and, more than anything else, to wire.' Upon receiving orders for a wiring party the site was surveyed by officers of the Battalion, who decided how many men could be employed on the task, the best points of exit from our front line trenches and the quantity of material required. Special arrangements had to be made with the troops on both flanks to ensure that they did not open fire by mistake upon our own men, not an unlikely happening in the darkness or in the excitement of an alarm. The wiring party proceeded from camp to a suitable dump where some of the men picked up say, half a dozen of the special twisted metal stakes, others took coils of barbed wire, wire cutters, Very lights and pistols, and special wiring gloves. Arriving in the front line, enquiries were made to make sure that proper patrols had been sent out into No Man's Land to cover our men whilst working, a most necessary precaution, for there was always the chance that enemy patrols were prowling about in the darkness and had they come upon us unawares they would most certainly have flung bombs into our midst. The officer in charge of the party then set out the stake carriers on the site and as fast as stakes were screwed into the ground other men ran out the barbed wire and fastened it securely to each stake. Everything had to be done as quietly as possible, no hammering or talking was permissible and whenever the enemy threw up a Very light, illuminating the vicinity for a couple of hundred yards, everyone had to keep perfectly still, whether standing or not, and remain still until the light had subsided. The most minute directions had to be given for guidance in case of hostile attack, but hostile fire, unless very intense, was not permitted to interfere with the energetic prosecution of the task, for on the soundness of the barbed wire obstacles depended to a great extent the security of the front.

B Company had the misfortune to suffer the loss of their company headquarters at 11 pm on the night of 29 June, when an incendiary shell fell upon the structure, which was very quickly burnt out. Sundry documents and papers of importance were destroyed in the conflagration, but it was understood that what gave the owners of the mess most sorrow was the disappearance in the flames of a couple of bottles of 'the old how d'ye do', a somewhat irreverent name for whisky invented, it is believed, by the Quartermaster. These incendiary shells were most unpleasant things. The Germans used two types against us, one was the ordinary 'carcass' type, filled with black powder and grease, the other, and a much more formidable variety, was filled with petroleum. When it burst it saturated the surrounding air with a cloud of fine petroleum spray. The result was an instantaneous blaze of great heat and extent, and anything at all inflammable was terribly burnt. We remembered seeing a team of five or six men, who had been serving a 60 pounder gun on the road side near Bailleul, when an incendiary shell had fallen full on the breech of the gun; all the poor fellows were writhing about on the ground, charred perfectly black.

From 1 July onwards all the companies of the Battalion were engaged on trench construction and tramway maintenance; both B and D Companies found it necessary to ask for the assistance of large working parties from the infantry. Each company sent a platoon back to L'Hofland for five days rest and general training, at the end of which time it went up to the line and another platoon was sent down. All this work was rendered necessary on account of information received to the effect that the enemy was making large concentrations of troops on our front. The intelligence sheets, in fact, reported arrivals of fresh divisions almost daily and it was evident that another attack on Hazebrouck and the coast was contemplated. This information was quite alarming since the Division was holding a wide front with very few troops in reserve. Comprehensive defence schemes were drawn up under which definite posts were allotted to all available troops and always the order included, 'Posts must be held to the last.' Arrangements were made for the destruction of bridges and cross roads, and we were informed of the date upon which the attack was expected. Excitement and anxiety fought for first place in our thoughts but, at the last moment, we were told that the enemy had postponed his projected assault. Again and again we were informed of postponements and finally we were greatly relieved to learn of the withdrawal of many of the concentrated enemy divisions in consequence of the offensive launched by the British further south.

To our relief we heard on 22 July that Lieutenants L. Forsdike and J.B. Wilson, both of whom had been missing after the action on 13 April, were officially accepted as prisoners of war in Germany. Nevertheless, we had heard quite enough about the terrible experiences of prisoners in German hands to make us feel not a little uneasy on their account. Second-Lieutenant T.B. Clarke had also been wounded and taken prisoner at the same time, and the story of his experiences makes interesting reading and is set out below.

One of the possibilities of which I never dreamed during the war was that of being captured, but on April 13th, 1918, I was wounded in the leg near Vieux Berquin and within a few moments of being hit I was behind the advancing Boche front line. As I spent most of my period of captivity in bed, I saw very little of Germany, the first three months being spent in hospital at Lille. From there I was moved, via Tournai and Aachen, to Dortmund in Westphalia, where I was another month in hospital and then by passenger train to Karlsruhe in Baden, where I was in camp for three weeks before being sent to another camp in Kamstigall bei Pillau, in East Prussia. In the course of these journeys I was able to see something of the country in the last two only. It was a most delightful trip from Dortmund down the Rhine valley to Karlsruhe, and an equally un-delightful journey from Karlsruhe to East Prussia, due, no doubt, to the fact that we took four days over it and got only one meal per day. These different hospitals and camps varied considerably. That at Lille was an immense school turned into a hospital and very poorly fitted up. The food was miserable, consisting of very little besides black bread and dried vegetable soup, and the staff was quite inadequate, there being no sisters, only one doctor, and perhaps two or three orderlies for 200 wounded men. The chief thing we had to complain about was neglect rather than bad treatment. We were taken very little notice of, our wounds were dressed once a week at the most and very often at much longer periods, and we had no facilities at all for keeping clean. There was no hot water and no baths, and we had just a bowl of cold water brought to us every morning.

Unlike British hospitals, every dressing was done in the theatre, and this was merely a dirty room furnished with nothing else but a couple of operating tables. The doctor certainly worked under difficulties, being short of both instruments and anaesthetics, but in spite of this several unnecessarily cruel and inhuman operations were done. For instance, one morning I sat on one operating table waiting my turn to be dressed whilst on the next table they amputated a man's arm without an anaesthetic, cursing the poor fellow continuously for not keeping quiet! He died before they finished, so they left him to come to me. The hospital at Dortmund, however, was quite unlike this. The food was excellent, sanitary arrangements also, and there were plenty of doctors, sisters and other staff, in fact, ample to have spared a few for Lille! The town itself, too, unlike Lille, seemed to be thriving and to have no lack of good food. The Boche had, apparently, a very extraordinary and callous way of dealing with his own wounded, too, not bothering to help a seriously wounded man much because, as the doctor told me, he would be of no use in the line again. The result was that limbs which could have been restored to nearly normal in time were just patched up in the easiest way possible, leaving the man unnecessarily a cripple for life. As to my personal treatment, I suppose, compared with many other prisoners, I was well off, for I had a bad wound and the leg is now pretty sound, although it was not until I arrived in England that I was able to get it clean and healed after thirteen operations. The camp life was to me not very different from hospital, as I spent most of the time in bed being unable to walk. The best time of my captivity was spent at Karlsruhe, which was a big distributing centre for prisoners of all nationalities. The food was good there, and on account of the camp having been running since the beginning of the war it was exceedingly well organised and had a library, billiard room, canteen, etc. Cards seemed to be the chief form of recreation, and the monotony of this was broken by some amusing incidents. For instance, one evening a Canadian officer coming out of the canteen after a lengthy evening with the good Rhine wine spotted the German sergeant-major, whom everyone hated for his objectionable and officious manner. Letting out his war cry, the Canadian rushed at the sergeant-major and knocked him down. Things might have ended badly for the officer as the sergeant-major drew his sword and attacked him, but fortunately some Englishmen standing by held them both back. The sequel was five days confinement to cells for the Canadian. A few days later the same man (again after making acquaintance with the Rhine wine) mounted a donkey that was grazing in the grounds of the camp. After going twice round the grounds the donkey objected and threw him off through the window of the Boche commandant's hut. Result, another five days. The last camp in Kamstigall differed from this in every respect. There were about 900 of us, 300 of whom only were wounded, and we were sent from Karlsruhe to form this new camp, which seemed to be almost beyond the borders of civilisation – bitterly cold, very little food, only one blanket per man and nothing to do except play cards when it was possible to obtain a pack to play with, which was seldom, as there were only the few packs that had been brought with us, say about a dozen amongst 900 fellows.

A few words about the organisation of pay, letters and parcels. The system of pay was to allow each officer forty marks per month, or if in hospital twenty marks only, the other twenty being taken for board and lodging. This charge was debited to each officer's account at his Army bankers. As I was moved about a good deal during the time I was a prisoner I did not get all my pay through, though it was, I found afterwards, debited to my account with Cox's alright. [Cox & Co. was the bank used by the KOYLI and many, if not all, of its officers.] Letters I only got through three weeks before I left Germany, and of the many parcels I had sent to me not one reached me! The prisoners who had been captured twelve months or over, in most cases, got parcels pretty regularly, and letters too. They were sent out via Switzerland and Holland. We got very little news at most places, though an official news bulletin was issued in the larger camps. Being a German version it was nearly always the same, 'Great German victory at...'. I left Kamstigall on December 9th 1918, and one of the best moments of my whole life was when I landed at Leith and I was able to realise the prisoner's life was all over.

The close of the month found us still working away on the defences and in reviewing the month's work we came to the conclusion that B Company appeared to have had by far the worst time; their defences at Swartenbrouck were continuously shelled and, as already related, their headquarters was burnt out. Lance Corporal E. Blanchard was prominent throughout the period by reason of his courage and general devotion to duty and was rewarded with the Military Medal, an honour well deserved. Battalion HQ moved to La Cunewele, a quiet spot west of Hazebrouck, on 10 August and work as usual continued up to 25 August; on this date 40th Division relieved 31st Division and we handed our territory over to 17th Battalion, Worcestershire Regiment. Our respite from labour was, however, extremely brief, amounting to a few hours only, for no sooner was this relief completed than we immediately proceeded to relieve 9th Division, next in line to the north in the Meteren sector. The Battalion took over from 9th Seaforth Highlanders, and HQ occupied their old site at Alum Farm, near Caestre. B Company, which was working on rear roads, accompanied them. C Company went to Thieushouk and worked on forward roads and trenches, while D Company took over Tyler's Farm on the outskirts of Caestre and commenced the construction of a light railway. This marked the beginning of the final phase of the War.

Chapter 10

Work in the Meteren sector – Retirement of the enemy – A strenuous time on the road work – Attack on Ploegsteert and Warneton – Honours and Awards – Crossing of the Lys – We enter Roubaix – Rumours of an Armistice – Move on to Renaix – More Honours and Awards

For five days we carried on with the various tasks listed at the close of the last chapter, but on 31 August (1918) great excitement was caused by the news that the enemy had retired from Bailleul. B and C Companies were immediately put on opening up roads leading into the town. They had the assistance of no fewer than 800 men from infantry units and by 6 pm that day they had cleared the main road through Meteren and Bailleul. This was a very creditable piece of work, at least so said the general and several other officers whose units had used the road. The whole of the next week was a particularly trying one for the Battalion. The urgent necessity for opening up forward communications with the very least possible delay involved very heavy work, but our wonderful Yorkshire lads went at it like Trojans, and the rate of progress was such that all companies had to move forward almost daily. The Battalion strength on 1 September was twenty-six officers and 749 other ranks (including attached), as compared with thirty-one officers and 988 men the day we arrived at Hallencourt.

But now we must go back a little way and consider what was happening on other parts of the front, and why the German retreat from our own sector was made. [The Germans believed they had delivered a crushing blow to what they called the 'Entente Front' – the French and British Armies from Amiens north to the Hazebrouk area.] In the early days of July the Germans launched a great attack against the French on the Champagne-Marne front. This attack was to be the great 'peace assault', as Ludendorff put it, and was in fact Germany's dying effort. This second attack failed, and the German commander sought, by withdrawing part of his line behind the River Marne, to gain time for pushing on his preparations for the great 'Hargen' attack in Flanders. Hardly had arrangements been made for this when, on the morning of 18 July, Marshal Foch's flank attack fell upon him at Soissons, and this proved to be the turning point of the war. As von Hertling, the German Chancellor, has written, 'on the 18 [July] even the most optimistic among us understood that all was lost'. Ludendorff on hearing of the reverse at Soissons realized at once the threatening consequences to his armies, and immediately proceeded to Avesnes to arrange for the necessary withdrawal from the Marne salient.

Meanwhile, on 8 August, the brilliant attack on the Amiens salient was delivered by Field Marshal Haig. The German troops holding the salient were over-run and practically exterminated. Ludendorff called this Germany's 'black day', and in fact so grave was the crisis felt to be that a conference of army leaders and members of the German Cabinet was held at Spa on 13 August, at which it was agreed that further prosecution of the war was hopeless and that peace should be sued for whenever a temporary improvement in Germany's military position occurred. This battle was followed by a great French attack between the Oise and the Aisne, and then the British Third Army attacked on the line Bapaume – Péronne. Both attacks exceeded all expectations in the results achieved, and the scales dropped from the eyes of the German soldier. The German reserves steadily dwindled, munitions and supplies lessened, and morale evaporated almost entirely. Foch, however, had other surprises in store for France's hereditary enemies. [On 26 March, when the British and French armies were retreating following the German offensive of 21 March, the Allies announced that the French General Foch had been given responsibility for co-ordinating all Allied Armies on the Western Front.] The agreed plan was for the British to break through the Hindenburg line in the direction of Cambrai – St. Quentin – Arras, while the French and Americans were to rupture the German defences north of Verdun and advance on Mezières. [General Foch's offensive strategy, in July 1918, proposed a series of surprise attacks, with short intervals between each, which would drive the Germans away from the Channel ports and regain the coal mining areas of Northern France.

The initial attack, on 8 August, was aimed at pushing the Germans back in the section of the front line before Amiens. Cambrai, St Quentin and Arras would eventually feature in the plan but were not an objective in the initial operation.] Having already suffered great losses in men and material; and with the need to preserve his dwindling forces, coupled with the fact that his left flank was being pushed eastwards, Ludendorff was forced to withdraw the German troops from our front on 31 August. Their withdrawal was made slowly and in good order, yet losses on both sides were equally severe. The whole German Army fell back to the so-called Hindenburg line or, as the Germans themselves called it, the Siegfried Stellung, where they hoped to gain time to reorganize the depleted units.

On our front, the advance having been stopped by the enemy about Ploegsteert (of unhappy memory) on 6 September, our camps became again more or less settled, with Battalion HQ established just east of Bailleul, and the companies camped a little in the rear of Neuve Eglise. Our work at this time was mainly repairing forward roads and erecting screens to shield traffic on these roads from direct enemy observation. The roads had been mined in many places by the retreating enemy, and the work of repair was both dangerous and arduous. In order to keep companies supplied with materials, the Transport Officer found it necessary to employ ten GS (General Service) waggons, eight tip carts, and twenty-one motor lorries.

Meanwhile, on 9 September, a few miles from us at Cassel, a conference between the British, Belgian and French commanders-in-chief was arranged at which a fourth offensive was planned to take place on the extreme left flank, with the objective of forcing the Germans back on Ghent. This offensive, however, was not to begin until 28 September. In the interval, we as a unit carried on with our allotted tasks and performed wonders in road building. Then, on the appointed day, the attack was launched, with 31st Division attacking Ploegsteert Wood and the village of Warneton. The attack was splendidly successful and the enemy was driven back to the line of the river Lys. In these operations, D Company, Captain W. Baird, MC, was attached to a mobile column of 93 Infantry Brigade, and rendered very valuable assistance in opening up forward roads, all of which were in an indescribable condition. The 28 September was an important date in another respect, for it was on that day that Ludendorff and Hindenburg at last accepted the situation and agreed that for them the end had come, and the next day the German Foreign Minister was informed of their army's desperate plight. On 1 October, Hindenburg and the Kaiser went together to Berlin (one can imagine the melancholy conversation carried on between these two during the journey) and on 4 October the first peace offer was sent to President Wilson. When the attack of 28 September was all over, Battalion HQ moved forward to De Broeken Road, near Neuve Eglise, and each company headquarters also made a move forward. [De Broeken Road may be the Battalion's bi-lingual form of 'the road to Broekenhoek, a small town south-east of Kortrijk (French, Coutrai).] Work on roads was resumed. The enemy dropped an occasional shell in our direction, chiefly shrapnel, but only one or two men were wounded and, as it happened, this was our last experience of being under fire. On 4 October, we had news that twenty-one men, who had been missing after the action on 13 April near the Rue du Bois, had been officially reported as prisoners of war in Germany. Lieutenant Colonel C.B. Charlesworth rejoined for duty on 10 October and took command from Major G.M. Stockings. For services rendered in the previous six months the following awards were announced in the New Year Honours List, 1919:-

Mentioned in Dispatches:
Lieutenant J. Downs
Lieutenant H. G. Meek
Sergeant E. Chappell
Sergeant W. Wardle

The following were awarded the Croix de Guerre
Captain W. Baird, MC
Sergeant J. Ellis, MM
Corporal A. Jagger

Individual award:
Private W. White DCM

By this time the enemy was in full retreat on his entire front from the Scheldt to the Aisne, and Foch ordered the British Armies to push on towards Mons and Avesnes in conjunction with a French advance on the right. On 16 October, Battalion HQ moved forward to The Piggeries, near Warneton, a small town on the Belgian-French frontier. [Warneton is on the Belgian-French frontier, but the Piggeries must be a Battalion term for a badly sighted camp nearby.] B and C Companies established their headquarters in the town itself, while D Company shifted forward to Quesnoy-sur-Deûle. Whilst here Lieutenant Colonel C.B. Charlesworth was unfortunately seized with illness, Major G.M. Stockings taking over the command again. All our men were busily engaged preparing for the crossing of the Lys. Every bridge had been destroyed by the enemy, who was holding the eastern bank of the river, which provided a considerable obstacle. From Armèntieres to Menin the Lys is, of course, the boundary between Belgium and France. Before any serious attempt to cross the river could be made, all the main roads leading to it had to be made fit for heavy transport and great quantities of materials for bridge construction had to be brought up in readiness for the crossing. All bridge heads of any consequence were naturally under desultory long range fire. Large parties from the Battalion under the orders of the OC 210th and 211th Field Companies, Royal Engineers, were working on Warneton and Pont Rouge bridges and their approaches, whilst other parties, assisted by men from the divisional infantry, worked on the main roads. Early on the morning of 18 October the infantry crossed the Lys and found that the enemy had retired for a considerable distance, whereupon Battalion HQ moved forward to Quesnoy-sur-Deûle, and D Company, ever in the forefront, went east to Bondues. As a matter of fact, on several occasions during this pursuit D Company was actually ahead of our own infantry. They were among the first troops to enter the town and were received with rapture by the inhabitants, who fell upon their necks with joy, much to the disgust of some of the old campaigners, who disliked such emotional outbursts. The actual conditions of the fighting are best understood by referring to the German reserves. When the attack of 28 September was begun, the Germans had sixty-nine divisions in reserve, yet by 15 October these had been reduced to twenty-six, of which only nine were rested. Of the divisions in the line, many were unfit for combat but could not be replaced. Again, on 19

October, the Battalion HQ moved, this time to Croix, a suburb of Roubaix, B and D Companies accompanying. Lieutenant Colonel C.B. Charlesworh rejoined here from hospital and took over the command from Major G.M. Stockings. C Company remained at Quesnoy to complete their work on the bridge there, rejoining the Battalion on 20 October. B Company went to Leers Nord on 19 October, and worked at various jobs under the command of 210th Field Company, Royal Engineers. On 21 October, Battalion HQ and C and D Companies moved to nice comfortable billets in Lannoy, passing on their way through Roubaix. This town was the centre of the great textile district of northern France and held a large colony of Yorkshire people, who gave our men a wildly enthusiastic welcome.

For the next few days the Battalion was engaged on preparations for the crossing of the River Escaut (Flemish – Scheldt) but, on 27 October orders were received to move into the XIX Corps area. The Battalion, therefore, marched first of all to Mouscron, billeting there for the night, and then to Staceghem. On 29 October Companies were working hard on roads that were in a bad state. The Germans had mined them in many places, and had also placed on them what obstructions they could, such as old vehicles, trees and assorted masonry. The enemy put up a stiff resistance on the east bank of the Escaut, which was naturally a very strong tactical position, and it required repeated attacks by the Division, extending over four days, to dislodge him. C Company had moved forward to Vichte on 30 October, to be in readiness for these operations. [Vichte is a small village to the east of Kortrijk, Belgium.]

The Allied armies began their final drive on 1 November and, playing its small part in the general scheme, the Division attacked Audenarde (Flemish – Oudenarde) on that date. Each company of the Battalion was attached to a Field Company of the Royal Engineers and most valuable work was done in keeping communications open. At Audenarde we were on historic ground for it was here that the decisive Battle of Audenarde was fought (11 July, 1708) between the English forces under the Duke of Marlborough and Prince Eugene of Savoy, and the French commanded by Vendôme, which resulted in such disaster for the French. The 31st Division became Corps Reserve on 3 November, and the Battalion then moved to Halluin [a suburb of Menin], where general training and re-fitting was done, a very enjoyable period to be sure. Then, on 7 November, as the Division had again taken over a sector of the front, we marched eastward to Marcke [a suburb of Kortrijk], and stayed the night there. The next day we wandered into Sweveghem, [Zwevegem south-east of Kortrijk], only five miles away, and were billeted in a power station. The Germans had taken away everything portable and had wrecked the machinery that was too heavy to shift. Preparations were now under way for an attack on the enemy's position upon the high ground on the other side of the Scheldt around Rugge, and all our men were cooperating with the Royal Engineers on approaches and bridges over the river. [Today, Captain England's town of Rugge is a small modern settlement either side of the road from Avelgem to Kluisbergen, near the border with France. It is close to the River Scheldt, which the French call the Escaut, and the high ground to be attacked was possibly Mont de l'Enclus.] The attack was to take place on 10 November, but the Germans retired the day before and saved us the trouble of consuming large quantities of ammunition. However, the preparations were not entirely wasted for we were able to throw a bridge across in very quick time, allowing patrols to push forward and keep in touch with the fleeing enemy.

On 10 November Battalion HQ moved to Oroir, a small town just east of the confluence of the rivers Rosne and Escaut; B and C Companies were still at Rugge and D Company moved to Amougies, once again in the van; good old D Company! This same night we heard strong rumours that an armistice was to be declared at 11am the next morning, but the thing seemed altogether too good to be true. We had got so accustomed to battle and sudden death that the prospect of peace seemed far too remote to be worth consideration. Our feelings were also tinged with a little disappointment for the simple reason that, having got the Boche on the run at long last, it was our great desire to pursue him to the gates of Berlin itself. However, second thoughts were best, and there was much jollification in the Battalion that night, and indeed in all battalions, especially when it was found definitely that the cease fire was to sound at 11 am on the following day.

We awoke on 11 November – 'A momentous day' with light hearts and heavy heads – the vin blanc no doubt. Then, we marched to Renaix and received a civic welcome from the inhabitants, who were almost delirious with joy at their release after four years of blood and iron. For services rendered during the final phase the following awards were made:

Major D. E. Roberts, MC	Croix de Guerre (Belgian).
Private E. Dawson	Croix de Guerre (Belgian).
Private G. Webster	Croix de Guerre (Belgian).

In the final Peace Dispatch the following honours were awarded:

Sergeant C. Fairhurst	Distinguished Conduct Medal.
Sergeant F. Q. Walters	Distinguished Conduct Medal.
Captain N. L. Bennett	Mentioned in Dispatches.
Captain W. Parkin	Mentioned in Dispatches.
Captain G. R. Atkinson	Mentioned in Dispatches.
CSM A. Hull	Mentioned in Dispatches.
Sergeant Firth	Mentioned in Dispatches.
Corporal (acting Sergeant) H. Marlow	Mentioned in Dispatches.
Private R. G. Hiorns	Mentioned in Dispatches.
Private C. W. Sharman	Mentioned in Dispatches.

Chapter 11

Renaix. The 'TYKES' concert party – We commence our march home – Presentation of medals – Demobilization begins – We have a pleasant time at St Omer – Presentation of Colours at Blendecques – Cadre leaves France – Arrives at Ripon – Colours deposited at Wakefield Town Hall – Demobilization of the cadre

At Renaix we found comfortable billets and the inhabitants positively fell over themselves to do us favours. The whole town was en fête; from secret hiding places were produced bunting and flags, all carefully stored up during the German occupation against the day of deliverance. Bands of young men and women, and old ones too, marched up and down the streets laughing and singing the popular [French] military air 'Madelon', while we officers and men alike flirted outrageously with the damsels of the place and made pretty speeches in halting French, little of which was understood. Unlike the people of other places where we had stayed, these folk, having been behind the German lines, had picked up no English.

On 12 November B Company went forward to Everbecq, where they came under the orders of the GOC, 92 Brigade, which was on outpost duty. The remainder of the Battalion did occasional parades, played much football and held sports, but all our conversation was of peace and home. Whilst at Renaix, the Battalion Concert Party, which went under the name of 'The Tykes', gave its first performance. The party, we believe, was originally organised by Captain P.C. Binns and Lieutenant J. Downs, and was an extremely good one, being ably stage-managed by Lieutenant L.F. Philips. Many shows were given in various places and for each performance the stalls were five francs, the pit was two francs, and the gallery one franc; curiously, the 'gallery'

12th KOYLI football team. The officer on the left with the black armband is Major D.E. Roberts.

stood round the sides and at the back. Second Lieutenant J. A. Grayson was the Battalion 'Lady' and, when seen from afar off, made a most realistic one. Lieutenant J. Downs was dispatched to Paris with instructions to bring back a complete outfit of clothes for the 'lady', down to the smallest detail, and he fulfilled his mission nobly, though we understand he experienced great difficulty regarding the size of the garments. In this connection a comical incident occurred. The daughter of the house where C Company officers were billeted had just returned from Paris, and someone (Captain Binns and Lieutenant Downs are pointed out as the culprits) conceived the idea of persuading this girl to appear with our Concert Party in place of Second Lieutenant Grayson. However, she needed but little persuasion and, as she had a good voice, played the piano well, and knew all the latest songs, both French and English, she went on straightaway and there were no problems. In due course she appeared on the stage and scored a great success, but unhappily some ASC (Army Service Corps) officers fell hopelessly in love with the maiden and they clustered round the stage door awaiting her exit. When she did appear she had to be escorted home by a bodyguard for protection against the lovesick swains of the ASC. The fame and beauty of this lady quickly circulated and at the next performance numerous ASC officers turned up from far and wide. Unfortunately for them, the real lady was not appearing, having done her very last performance the night before. Her place had been taken by Second Lieutenant Grayson but 'love is blind' and the officers of the ASC saw only the beauteous damsel who had captured their hearts the previous night. No escort was provided on this occasion. 'Miss' Grayson sat on a form surrounded by a bevy of dashing young gallants, made great play with 'her' eyes, ogling first one and then another, and by a judicious mixture of coyness and daring led on these poor lovers until each one was almost ready to blow out his brains for her. History does not reveal what happened when they finally discovered the deception.

We heard on 13 November that the Division had not been selected to go to Germany with the Army of Occupation and on the same day we moved west to Amougies and the start of the first stage of our journey home. On 14 November, we set off back to Sweveghem, and on the following day continued to Knocke, a very small hamlet between Menin and Kortrijk, where we remained until the 24 November training and cleaning-up generally. [This hamlet does not appear on modern maps.] Two days after we got to Knocke (17 November), there was a special Brigade Thanksgiving Service, to which we sent eight officers and 200 men. The service was rather impressive, and it perhaps made us realise more than anything else that the long, long war was really over at last. C Company had a real peace time job on 23 November, nothing more or less than the manufacture of tables, forms, desks and other scholastic paraphernalia destined for use in army school rooms. Later that day the Division was ordered to proceed to the St. Omer area, and on the following day the Battalion moved on to Menin. The march

The 31st Division's Visual Signal Section, Renaix, 13 November 1918. Only one of these men – centre back row – is wearing the Pioneer collar badge.

to Ypres continued the next day along that notorious road between Menin and Ypres that was known and hated by thousands of British lads who, in the dark dreary and unforgettable past, had tramped wearily along its fire-swept surface to take their chance in the death-filled trenches in front of Ypres. Oh, if inanimate things could speak what ghastly tales of poison gas and pitiless storms of shot and shell could those scarred fragments of the Menin Road relate; those blasted stumps which had once been trees, and what accounts of heroism unseen and unrewarded. Such thoughts passed through one's mind as one entered the shadow of Ypres, once the fairest town of Flanders, now a miserable wreck of stones and timber. Here we billeted for the night on the ramparts. On 26 November, we marched to Abeele and on the following day to Staple, another old friend. This, however, was not our final destination and, like John Brown's soul which went marching on, so did we to Quelmes, five and a half miles the other side of St. Omer. This was the last place in France in which the Battalion, as a complete unit, was billeted, and though there was joy in the camp, for many good and weighty reasons, yet there was also a tinge of sadness and regret at the thought that very soon we were to be dispersed to the four corners of the earth.

On 1 December 1918 the effective strength of the Battalion was forty-one officers and 843 other ranks (including attached); for purposes of comparison we may mention that the strength on 11 March 1918, the day we marched into Hallencourt, was thirty-one officers and 988 men. Many changes had occurred since then and whilst a number of those present at Hallencourt

The ammunition bandoliers worn by this group suggest they are from 12th KOYLI Transport Section and were responsible for both mechanical and horse-drawn vehicles.

were still with us at Quelmes, too many had paid the greatest price that man can pay but we did not forget them when the fighting was done and the battle won. Perhaps they were with us, unseen and unheard. Who knows?

For the first eleven days of December 1918 we occupied ourselves with a little training and some elaborate sports, which created great excitement. The Divisional Commander inspected us on 10 December, and presented medals. On the following day the first batch of men for demobilization left us, twenty men under Group III, and thereafter large parties left the Battalion daily en route for Blighty and home. We had a large proportion of coal miners in our ranks and these men were in the first class to be released. Industry in England had to be restarted before the bulk of the armies could be demobilized, but industry needed coal above everything else.

The Battalion, or what was left of it, moved on 17 December to the pleasant little town of Lumbres, on the St Omer – Boulogne road and, since no officers had left the Battalion for demobilization at this time, the opportunity was

Taken at Lumbres, on the road from St Omer to Boulogne, this last photograph taken in France shows Lieutenant Colonel C.B. Charlesworth (with black armband) and the officers of 12th KOYLI. Major W.G. Charlesworth is holding the dog 'Ginger'.

taken of securing a final photograph. Major W.G. Charlesworth is shown fondly clutching a small dog known as 'Ginger'. This little animal had come with a draft of reinforcements when the transport was at Borre on 11 of April 1918, and came on the strength during the lunch hour. Finding our fare better than anyone else's he stuck to us and was officially adopted by the HQ Mess and became the pet and mascot of the Battalion. When leaving France for England, Major Charlesworth wanted to take him home, but quarantine regulations did not permit this.

For the remainder of December officers and men were leaving us every day and by 1 January 1919 our strength had been reduced to 614 men and further reductions meant that by 31 January we only had thirty-six officers and 431 other ranks. The New Year Honours List appeared on 1 January and it is not an exaggeration to state that every officer and man was pleased to learn that our popular commanding officer, Major G.M. Stockings, had been honoured with the Companionship of the Distinguished Service Order and was also mentioned in dispatches. Towards the end of February, Lance Sergeant E. Parker and Private J. Redford were both awarded the Military Medal for consistent good work and devotion to duty. On 23 February, nine officers, thirty-one NCOs and fifteen privates received Divisional Badges and Parchments. On 7 February, the Battalion moved to St. Omer and had what is vulgarly called a posh time, meaning no shells, no bombs, hardly any parades, lovely weather, nice billets in a quaint old market town – what more could we hope for? Colours were presented to the Battalion with elaborate ceremony at 11 am on 19 February by Brigadier General G.B.F. Smyth, DSO, RE, and at the same time consecrated at a special parade service held at Blendecques. The Colour Party, whose names must be recorded as the chief participants in what was not only a grand spectacle but an important occasion in the Battalion's history, consisted of Lieutenant T. Downs, Sergeant Watherstone, Sergeant McFarthing, Corporal Thorne and Corporal Gott, with Major D.E. Roberts MC as Senior Major, while we must not forget to mention CSM Webb, who drew the Colours from the Adjutant prior to the ceremony. The concluding paragraph of Battalion Orders covering this event stated, 'The Battalion will march back to billets at the slope with Colours flying… '. Imagine the sadly depleted Battalion swinging along the high road in the fresh, crisp air of February, rifles at the

A few years older, but very much wiser, Major D.E. Roberts (extreme left) and four other 12th KOYLI officers some time after the Armistice had been signed.

slope, bayonets brightly gleaming in the sun, and at our head the symbols of our military faith, the Union Jack of old England proudly fluttering and flapping in the breeze. [Captain England's flight into jingoistic language can be excused on this occasion. He had been present at Serre on 1 July 1916; he had seen much that day and the sentiments he was now expressing would not have been present shortly after that action. He had survived three years on the Western Front and witnessed much of what today is believed to be responsible for numerous cases of post traumatic stress disorder. He had been there, he had seen the horrors of war, yet he still felt able to respond in this way shortly after the fighting had stopped. It is difficult to argue a case against his sentiments.]

For the benefit of the lay reader it can be here explained that each Battalion has two colours, the King's and the Regimental, the former being a Union Jack, while the latter bears the regimental crest surrounded with the regiment's battle honours. They both measure 3ft. 9in. by 3ft. and are of fine silk, elaborately edged with a gold fringe and gold and crimson tassels. Colours nowadays are not taken into action; and it is interesting to note that the practice of leaving them behind on taking the field dates only from the battle of Isandhlwana in 1879, when two promising young officers lost their lives trying to save the colours of the 24th Regiment of Foot [now the 24th Regiment, together with the 41st Regiment, form the Royal Regiment of Wales].

By the middle of February we still numbered about 200 men but, as these were retainable in the Army of Occupation, they were drafted to other units. By the middle of April the Battalion was reduced to its Cadre strength of five officers and forty men, and it was this party that was retained to take home the Battalion transport, stores, papers and the colours. Some of the units raised for the war were disbanded when peace came, their records being sent to England, and their memory effaced from official records. Not so with 12th Battalion, King's Own Yorkshire Light Infantry for, on 25 March, we had the gratifying news that ours was one of the battalions whose identity was to be preserved. There were some who thought this merely a wise precaution until all stores had been finally accounted for, a sentiment which we considered an insult to our good name as Yorkshiremen. The Cadre marched to Wizernes on 2 April: the 31st Division began to entrain for England on 13 May, and the remnants of the Battalion took train at 1 pm, 19 May 1919, for Dunkirk. They embarked on HMT *Mocoleff*, and at 4 pm in the afternoon of 24 May sailed for England, arriving at Ripon (Yorks) in the early morning of the 27 May.

On 28 May the Cadre proceeded to Wakefield and with proper ceremonial Lieutenant T.E. Oxley handed the colours over to the Mayor of Wakefield (the late Alderman G. Blakey, OBE). They were deposited in the Town Hall, where they still remain and may be seen hanging in the Council Chamber.

Finally, all the transport and mobilization stores having been duly handed in, the Cadre was itself demobilized on 2 June 1919 and thus ended for 12th Battalion, King's Own Yorkshire Light Infantry – 't'owd Twelfth' – its glorious adventure.

This photograph is believed to show the 12th KOYLI cadre marching to Wakefield Town Hall for the ceremony of presenting the Battalion's Colours to the Mayor of Wakefield.

Lieutenant T.E. Oxley about to present the King's Colour to the Mayor of Wakefield, Alderman G.E. Blakey OBE, with Lieutenant Colonel C.B. Charlesworth, commanding the parade, 28 May 1919.

Chapter 12

The Battalion's Casualties – Some Interesting Figures – Conclusion

W hen the Armistice was sounded on 11 November 1918, the Battalion had been officially mobilised for four years and one week. During that time three officers and 216 non-commissioned officers and men had died whilst serving with the Battalion, either in action against the enemy or from disease incurred while on military service. A complete list of our comrades who lost their lives during the Great War is included in this history.

It will be useful to include in a history of this kind a few facts and figures which will serve as a reminder of the titanic character of the struggle in which 12th Battalion KOYLI played its part so well. In August 1914, the total strength of the British Army in all theatres of action was 733,514 of all ranks; this includes the Army Reserve, the Special Reserve, the Territorial Force, and other units. In November 1918, this figure had grown to the colossal total of 8,654,467, made up as follows:

Strength in August, 1914	733,514
Recruited during the war:-	
England	4,006,158
Scotland	557,618
Wales	272,924
Ireland	134,202
Canada	628,964
Australia	416,809
New Zealand	220,099
Africa	136,070
Newfoundland	23,922
	7,130,280

Colonial Troops:	
Indian	1,401,350
South African	92,837
West Indian	10,000
Other Colonies	20,000
	8,654,467

(The War Cabinet, 1918, Comd. 235, p. 95).

The casualties were appalling and the flower of the world's manhood was swept away in millions. It does not seem possible to obtain exact figures. Different numbers have been published at different times. The table set out below is based on estimates prepared by the United States Army.

(*The Times*, 4 March, 1919), as amended by other authoritative figures (*The Times*, 3 Nov, 23, 28 December 1918; 9 April, 6 May, 2 Sept, 6 Nov, 1919. 26 March, 20 April, 18 June, 1920).

[No definitive lists of casualties exist for any of the countries involved in the First World War. Each country has produced its own estimates, but the exact numbers will never be known.]

Casualties among all the belligerents

	Killed including Missing, unless separately stated	Missing presumed dead	Wounded	Total
ALLIES				
British Empire	765,483	108,346	2,090.989	2,964,818
Belgium	102,382	—	*200,000*	302,382
France	1,358,872	361,654	2,750,000	4,470,526
Italy	507,169	—	*1,000,000*	1,507,169
Portugal	8,367	—	16,000	24,367
Roumania	300,000	—	*300,000*	600,000
Russia	1,700,000	—	3,500,000	5,200,000
Serbia	300,000	—	*300,000*	600,000
United States	53,160	1,160	179,625	233,945
TOTALS	5,095,433	471,160	10,336,614	15,903,207

	Killed including Missing, unless separately stated	Missing presumed dead	Wounded	Total
CENTRAL POWERS				
Austria	800,000	—	3,200,000	1,000,000
Bulgaria	100,000	—	*200,000*	300,000
Germany	1,600,000	103,000	4,064,000	5,767,000
Turkey	250,000	—	*500,000*	750,000
Totals	2,750,000	103,000	7,964,000	10,817,000
GRAND TOTALS	7,845,433	574,160	18,300,614	26,720,207

NOTE. The figures in italics are round numbers calculated by allowing two wounded for each man killed or missing. This is, however, a conservative estimate as the usual proportion is 2½ or even 3 to 1. The conditions in Serbia and Roumania were exceptional and a still lower estimate of the proportion of wounded to killed has been adopted.

That is the price the world paid for liberty, and for our determination to honour our signature on 'a scrap of paper'. [The scrap of paper is a reference to Article 7 of the 1839 London Treaty made between Britain, France, Austria, Prussia and Russia on the one side and The Netherlands. All agreed that Belgium was to be a neutral state. When Germany violated the neutrality of Belgium in 1914, it effectively committed Britain to declare war on Germany in the defence of Belgium.]

Here is a very impressive statement. In August, 1914, the Royal Artillery personnel of the British Army throughout the world totalled 92,920, but by August, 1918, it had reached the vast total of 548,780. Over half a million men engaged solely on artillery work; truly, a stupendous figure. In 1914 there were no anti-aircraft batteries; in 1918 there were 275. Some remarkable figures relate to the Army Medical Services. For instance, over 108 million bandages were used, 87,700 miles of gauze and 7,250 tons of cotton wool and lint! When the war commenced hospital accommodation in the United Kingdom was some 7,000 beds distributed in 200 different hospitals; at the time of the Armistice no less than 364,133 beds were available in 2,426 hospitals. [It is not certain whether Captain England is referring to military hospitals exclusively, or to the overall number of hospitals and beds through the United Kingdom.] The strength of the Royal Army Medical Corps in 1914 was 1,068 officers and 3,895 other ranks; in November, four years later, this strength had risen to 13,045 officers and 131,361 other ranks, not including 12,769 nursing sisters and 10,897 V.A.Ds. The RAMC supplied over 350,000 pairs of spectacles and 22,386 artificial eyes. Figures relating to the Royal Army Service Corps have been given in the body of the work. It might, however, be mentioned here that this branch of the service employed in Egypt 40,000 camels and 8,000 donkeys. The food supply was, of course, their most important work.

As the armies increased in size, and included many different nationalities among their personnel, special treatment in diet was required so that a remarkable diversity of commodities had to be provided; the number of these at the cessation of hostilities amounted to about 500 articles as compared with about sixty in 1914.

The Army Ordnance Service furnishes some staggering figures and some idea of the magnitude of the task imposed upon it can be had when it is stated that during the war the department dealt with 5,756 heavy guns (6 inch and larger) ; 21,160 field pieces (60 pounders and under); 230,000 machine guns; 217 million rounds of gun ammunition: 9,150 million rounds of small arms ammunition; 40,674,773 blankets; 6,500,000 sets of equipment; over 27 million tunics and the same number of trousers; 8 million pairs of pantaloons (or pants); and 40 million pairs of boots. [In March 1922, His Majesty's Stationery Office, HMSO, the War Office, published – Abstract of Official Statistics of the Military Effort of the British Empire During the Great War 1914–20. Captain England may well have used the data in this publication to compile the numerous figures he quotes above.]

But what of France, the country in which we passed so much of our time? The Germans invaded ten departments of France containing 6½ million inhabitants, the richest of all France in money, art, natural resources and historical associations. When the Armistice was declared this is the prospect which confronted the country. 1,400,000 people had been murdered by the Germans, in spite of the claims of 'Kultur'; 800,000 had been crippled and 3,000,000 wounded, quite apart from Army casualties. 4,000,000 hectares of land had to be put in order again; 265,000,000 cubic metres of trenches had to be filled in, and 300,000,000 square metres of barbed wire entanglements had to be pulled up.

Nearly 300,000 houses had to be completely rebuilt and the same number required extensive repairs. Shellfire had damaged 3,296 schools, 2,674 churches, 2,447 town halls (Mairies), and 49 hospitals.

The Germans had carried away no less than 523,000 milch [milk] cows, 469,000 sheep and goats, and 367,000 horses, donkeys and mules. Furthermore, 220 coal mines had to be re-constructed; the total damage done to the collieries being estimated at 880 million francs. Finally, over 3,500 industrial establishments of all kinds had been destroyed or badly damaged; two million families had been ruined; 2,700,000 had been driven from their homes – and that, people of England, is WAR.

Yet, terrible as these cold figures sound, they convey nothing whatever of the mental and bodily anguish suffered by the unfortunate people concerned, or the misery endured by hundreds of thousands of innocent children and aged and infirm men and women.

May such a dreadful calamity never fall upon our own country of England.

THE END

LIST OF OFFICERS, NON-COMMISSIONED OFFICERS AND MEN OF THE 12th KING'S OWN YORKSHIRE LIGHHT INFANTRY WHO DIED IN THE SERVICE OF THE COUNTRY

Second Lieutenant	M. Bingham	13-04-18
Lieutenant	J.S.L. Welsh	01-07-16
Captain	F.H. White MC	15-04-18
1359 Private	M. Able	01-07-16
34150 Private	J. Allison	13-04-18
1280 Private	E. Ambler	13-04-18
111 Private	G.H. Ambler	13-04-18
3 Corporal	J. W. Andrews	01-07-16
12/797 Private	S. Appleyard	06-04-17
37120 Private	R.E Archer	13-04-18
618 Private	S. Asprey	13-04-18
62134 Private	J. Barnes	08-12-18
1622 Private	T. Barnett	13-04-18
257 Lance Corporal	H. Bates	13-04-18
50041 Private	W. Baxter	13-04-18
235855 Private	D.T. Beaman	20-09-18
43653 Lance Sergeant	H.S. Bell	19-07-18
273 Sergeant	A. Bennett	13-04-18
92 Private	B. Bennett	14-04-18
49471 Private	E. Bennett	08-11-17
41768 Private	C.R. Bergen	13-04-1
12/1130 Private	A. Berry	26-12-15
1417 Private	R. Birkbeck	01-07-16
49296 Sergeant	C. Blythe	08-11-17
1185 Private	W. Bonnor	13-04-18
888 Private	E. Borland	28-06-17
1980 Private	B. Bottomley	13-04-18
34222 Private	C.H. Bray	13-04-18
99 Lance Corporal	W. Britton	08-05-17
3/1892 Private	W. Brown	17-04-18
1127 Private	E. Bryan	18-09-18

12798 Private	H.Bullock	05-08-18
1879 Private	J.M. Buxbury	13-08-18
730 Private	M. Calligan	22-10-17
3/1397 Private	F. Carey	30-03-18
36652 Private	J.L. Clark	13-04-18
732 Private	A.G. Carter	13-04-18
25360 Private	J. Chambers	25-03-18
51950 Private	G. Chapman	02-03-18
890 Private	A. Chennell	13-04-18
34225 Private	E. Chopping	12-05-17
17010 Private	J.T. Cogan	30-09-18
40252 Private	A. Cook	13-04-18
330 Private	F. Cooke	13-04-18
324 Private	J. Cording	21-06-18
1815 Private	A. Cornwell	13-04-18
204475 Private	N. Cozens	20-05-18
1099 Private	G H. Culshaw	14-04-18
51960 Private	W. Darley	02-07-18
1261 Private	T. Darnborough	01-07-16
338 Lance Corporal	W. Davies	13-04-18
37857 Lance Corporal	L. Dawson	08-10-17
1384 Private	G.A. Dean	07-04-17
904 Corporal	Derbyshire	15-10-17
1558 Private	H. Dews	01-07-16
903 Private	A. Donohoe	13-04-18
44210 Private	J. Driver	17-04-18
128 Private	J. Dunn	01-07-16
1788 Private	A. Duxbury	28-04-18
44194 Private	H. Dye	08-11-17
574 Corporal	Y. Eaton	13-04-18
907 Sergeant	F. Elliot	04-09-17
1514 Sergeant	E. Ellis	13-04-18
908 Corporal	J. Ellis	05-01-17
205201 Private	P. Ellis	29-11-17
49588 Private	W.E. Evans	31-10-17

1880 Private	C.W. Evinson	13-04-18
1006 Private	C. Farrer	28-04-18
51966 Private	J. Finney	04-07-16
1474 Private	J. Finnigan	01-07-16
34114 Private	A. Firth	03-04-18
1003 Private	H. Fisher	11-07-16
648 Private	T.H. Forrest	01-07-16
49486 Private	H.J. Forman	19-04-18
1504 Private	E. Foster	01-07-16
204671 Private	J. Frost	06-04-17
1009 Lance Corporal	J.J. Gardner	04-03-17
1858 Private	F. Garlick	22-08-18
1878 Private	B. Geary	01-07-16
375 Lance Sergeant	H. Gilbert	01-07-16
1194 Sergeant	N. Gomersall	12-05-17
104 Private	H. Greenhough	01-07-16
49491 Private	J. Griffen	13-04-18
661 Private	S. Halkyard	01-07-16
154 Private	F. Halstead	03-07-16
580 Private	G. Hayden	13-04-18
397 Private	F. Heald	13-04-18
1018 Private	S. Heaps	01-07-16
834 Private	R. Heaton	13-04-18
1197 Private	S. Heaton	13-04-18
833 Private	E. Heckingbottom	22-10-17
399 Private	E. Heptinstall	28-06-17
35584 Private	J. Herrod	29-06-17
1427 Private	A. Hewitt	01-07-16
1683 Private	H Hey	13-04-18
1987 Private	J. Higgins	11-05-17
402 Private	J. W. Hill	13-04-18
583 Private	E.W. Holmes	01-07-16
1464 Private	F. Holmes	01-07-16
101 Private	J. Holt	13-04-18
44216 Private	T. Horan	13-04-18

1424 Private	A. Horton	01-07-16
585 Sergeant	M. Hudson	04-03-17
750 Sergeant	T. Hughes	06-04-17
1162 Corporal	W.P. Humpherson	13-04-18
35946 Private	J. Jagger	15-10-17
37842 Private	? Jenkinson	13-04-18
20239 Private	G,E, Jerret	15-05-17
37844 Private	A.F. Johnson	27-03-18
46566 Private	H. Jones	13-04-18
420 Private	T. Jones	30-01-17
13057 Private	J.W. Jow	13-04-18
15 Private	J.C. Kaye	01-07-16
1418 Sergeant	J. Kilkenny	11-12-17
35588 Lance Corporal	C. Knighton	13-04-18
1507 Private	W.Langley	15-10-17
178 Private	G. Lapish	01-07-16
159 Private	G. Leek	01-07-16
437 Private	A. Lewis	13-04-18
45478 Private	H. Lewis	01-11-16
1573 Private	E. Lightfoot	12-07-16
1703 Private	G. Lodge	13-04-18
51995 Private	B. Lovick	02-07-18
102 Private	J. J. Luckman	13-11-16
675 Private	J. Lunt	12-06-18
676 Private	W.G. MacDonald	12-05-17
1785 Private	A.G. Malin	13-04-18
1412 Private	G.W. Marshall	13-04-18
2362 Private	H. Marshall	13-04-18
1037 Private	J. Marshall	13-04-18
22737 Private	J. McHugh	26-05-17
1785 Private	C. Micklethwaite	17-04-18
34254 Private	W.E. Middlebrook	06-02-17
23302 Private	J.R. Moakes	28-12-1
1450 Private	J.Moore	07-10-16
1041 Private	B. Mortimer	13-04-18

760 Sergeant	K. Moseley	04-07-16
1205 Lance Corporal	E. H. Moverley	30-06-18
1569 Private	A. Moyser	13-04-18
451 Private	W. Mulure	13-04-18
24707 Private	P. Murray	14-03-17
35963 Private	E. Newmarsh	23-10-17
1048 Private	C. Newton	10-06-16
194 Private	A. Ogden	12-05-17
37222 Private	J. T.Oldham	13-04-18
37834 Private	E. Oliver	13-04-18
44205 Private	A.W. Ounsworth	10-05-17
932 Private	J. Outram	01-07-16
1794 Private	W. Park	30-02-18
468 CSM	G.S. Parker DCM	13-04-18
1144 Lance Corporal	W. Parker	22-10-17
1262 Private	J. Parkes	13-05-18
197 Corporal	F. Parkin	30-08-17
34235 Private	H. Parkin	02-08-17
598 Corporal	A. Parson	18-09-17
2249 Private	J. Pendlebury	13-04-18
1367 Private	E. Pickles	12-07-16
204514 Private	F.G. Pinner	13-04-18
204515 Private	E.Potter	13-04-18
1321 Lance Corporal	C. Purdy	21-10-16
853 Private	J. Quin	25-03-18
1299 Private	W. Quinn	30-09-18
944 Lance Corporal	A. Ramsden	06-04-17
1057 Private	D. Ramsden	01-07-16
1298 Private	J. Randel	01-07-16
205586 Private	J. Richardson	23-04-18
34068 Private	J.W. Ruddleston	13-04-18
1469 Private	G.H. Ryan	06-04-17
49499 Private	O.T. Salt	08-11-17
37829 Private	A. Saunders	13-04-18
106 Private	T.W. Saville	13-04-18

1316 Private	A. Sayles	10-05-17
944 Lance Corporal	P.J. Schofield	01-07-16
860 Private	C. Smith	01-07-16
507 Lance Corporal	E. Smith	13-04-18
1066 Private	H. Smith	13-04-18
1063 Private	J. Smith	01-07-16
2204 Private	F. Squires	04-09-19
857 Private	J. Stephens	13-04-18
36661 Private	T. Stewart	13-04-18
1115 Private	B. Street	18-04-17
2151 Private	E. Sutcliffe	13-04-18
1071 Private	F. Sykes	13-04-18
1420 Private	J. Taylor	01-07-16
1540 Lance Corporal	J.W. Taylor	13-04-18
37869 Private	T.E. Taylor	07-04-17
37823 Private	W.H. Taylor	19-09-17
204482 Private	W. Terry	20-05-18
205168 Private	F. Thackery	04-09-17
529 Private	E. Tisdall	25-03-18
609 Private	G. Toddington	18-09-17
608 Private	J. Tomlinson	01-07-16
34058 Private	W.H. Torr	19-09-17
1215 Private	W.A. Trimbell	13-04-18
876 Lance Corporal	W. Wallace	31-07-16
228 Private	Walsh	01-07-16
537 Private	A. Ward	28-06-17
1369 Private	H. Ward	13-04-18
20452 Private	H. Warne	13-04-18
1555 Private	F. Watson	02-08-18
40314 Sergeant	H. Watson	12-07-18
1260 Private	J. Watson	13-04-18
1093 Private	J. Weate	01-07-16
1488 Private	A. Weaville	13-04-18
49590 Private	F.P. West	13-04-18
44755 Private	P.E. J. West	13-04-18

1836 Private	J. Wheater	13-04-18
877 Private	H. White	01-07-16
34086 Private	A. Whitaker	04-03-17
38293 Private	E. W. Whitfield	23-03-17
1281 Private	W.W. Wilde	10-07-16
551 Private	J. Williams	31-10-16
239 Private	J. Wilson	13-04-18
1675 Private	L. Wood	13-04-18
1648 Private	T. Wood	13-04-18
1087 Private	H. Woollen	24-04-18
37820 Private	A. Wright	13-04-18
229 Private	F. Wright	01-07-16

Note: This list is believed to be accurate but it is necessary to point out that a few of those reported missing were, afterwards found to be alive in Germany as prisoners of war. Unfortunately the records in our possession do not take cognisance of this fact and it is therefore possible that a few of the names are of individuals who were eventually repatriated.

Appendix I

Functions of a Pioneer Battalion

The true nature and functions of a pioneer battalion were never fully understood during the war, either by the military or laymen. The military authorities themselves could give us no definite information as to the scope of our duties. When we were officially appointed a pioneer battalion in 1915, the Commanding Officer sought authoritative advice on this subject, but he sought in vain. Consequently, it remained for us to discover as best we could what tasks we were most likely to encounter and we did this by studying the accounts of the great battles of the period and, perhaps with more profit, bv questioning closely our friends who had come back from the theatres of war.

We found that the average person had a vague idea that we were 'some sort of a labour battalion'. This was little short of an insult to both officers and men – to the former because most of them had been highly skilled engineers long before they joined the Army; to the latter because by no stretch of the imagination could they be regarded as either navvies or amateurs. Ninety-five per cent of our own men were coal hewers of long experience and were skilled exponents of the arts of shot-firing, the construction, use and maintenance of light railways and tramways, excavations in all materials and the erection of underground shelters of every description. All these things were part of their jobs in civilian life; in consequence they could be taught little or nothing in this respect. They were all perfectly well accustomed to long hours of physical exertion and from every point of view comprised human material of very fine quality; no better men for a pioneer battalion could possibly have been chosen.

Furthermore, the English coal miner is a great walker, and because of this characteristic our men were able to perform the most splendid marches. Entries in proof of this occur so frequently in the official War Diary that to make mention of even half of them would overload our history to the point of weariness. Having got hold of such a first rate body of men, it only remained for us to train them in military discipline and the use of a soldier's weapons. It has already been mentioned early in the book how quickly and thoroughly the men learnt these lessons and it is no idle boast when we say that in discipline, drill, and musketry exercises the 12th KOYLI stood second to no battalion in the whole 31st Division.

In a little booklet published in 1916 by Lieutenant L.S. Palmer of the Pioneer School of Instruction, this passage occurs:

'It is felt that no apology is needed for including a chapter on the Pick Axe; for not only is it the most useful of pioneer tools, but it is complementary to the rifle in the pioneer badge. A complete knowledge of this badge should always be the keynote of Pioneer training.'

There we have explained in a nutshell the goal at which we aimed continually – to be as efficient as infantry of the line in subjects purely military and to be the equal of the Royal Engineers in matters technical. That was our aim and object, but it was not so easy to carry it all into effect. Different commanders had different ideas of the purpose of a pioneer battalion. Some realised the worth of such a unit and did all they could to help us not only by providing us with comfortable quarters wherein it was possible to enjoy the rest so necessary if technical work is to be done properly, but also by exercising a wise discrimination as to the tasks we were to perform. Other commanders, with perhaps less experience in the use of pioneer troops, tended to set a much lower value on our services and the pioneers found themselves put on many jobs which could quite easily have been carried out by men not so highly skilled. The training and duties of modern infantry enable that arm to carry out much of the required defensive work without any skilled supervision or assistance and it is wasteful in the extreme to employ pioneers or engineers on tasks which non-technical troops can do quite well.

In fact, Major General Sir G. K. Scott-Moncrieff, writing in the Encyclopaedia Britannica, says of the pioneer battalions:

'It was not intended that these troops should be used as infantry except in the gravest emergency, although in some cases this was not borne in mind, and the resulting casualties made the want of such technical troops more acutely felt than ever.'

The same author, writing of the lessons to be learnt from the War, says:

'Then in the assault, the engineers should never be sent with attacking infantry except with specific instructions for definite work for which they can prepare beforehand. Even then they should not follow the leading waves of attack too closely as they get mixed up with the fighting line, and do not accomplish their actual work.'

In this and other quotations the term 'engineers' can be taken to be synonymous with 'pioneers', for to an increasing extent as the war progressed pioneer battalions became engineer units in all but name.

It is not possible to set out in full all the various tasks which fall to the lot of the pioneers in warfare.

The following summary gives a broad outline of their functions:

(a) They may be attached to attacking troops to wire and consolidate captured trenches and positions. In this case they follow the first line of the attackers, carrying with them their material.
(b) They may be detailed for the all-important work of opening up forward communications during or after the attack, in which event they would be a little way behind the first wave of the assaulting troops.
(c) In stationary, ie. trench warfare, they may be engaged on the construction of posts and trenches in the front line, the excavation of saps and erection of belts of barbed wire in No Man's Land, the excavation of deep dugouts or any other work within the trench system.
(d) When withdrawn from the trenches in stationary warfare they may he called upon to dig and wire rear defence systems, to make or repair rear roads and bridges, or works for the comfort, security and efficiency of the troops behind the line.
(e) In the case of a retreat in good order they would be employed mainly in delaying the pursuing enemy by means of demolitions and the erection

of obstacles. They may also have to take in hand the preparation of successive defensive positions.

(f)   In the case of a forced retreat in the presence of the enemy this obviously is a 'grave emergency', and pioneers would be called upon to act simply and solely as infantry of the line.

Those are, for all practical purposes, the general functions of a pioneer battalion. The letter which is printed below may, however, throw more light on this mysterious subject. It appeared in a newspaper during the war and is so amusing and, at the same time, strikes so many nails so squarely on the head that we feel no apology is needed for its insertion.

'In the old days we were long-whiskered gentry who, equipped with axes, marched at the head of the column. When the regiment was in quarters we did odd jobs about the place. Things are different now. The infantry erect their own camps and bivouacs – when they are lucky enough to have any. In this war we are the handy men of the British Army – the backbone of the Engineers' Services. What the R.E. haven't time or men enough to accomplish we do for them, an occasional scrap with the infantry varying the monotony. If the General decides to have a strong point at map location C.3d.16 he sends for his pet sapper, who says, 'Yes, certainly sir. I'll have it done at once.' Then he proceeds to indent for two companies of the Purston Pioneers to do the job for him.

Should the Brigadier decide to reclaim some ancient malodorous and water-logged support trenches, he suggests to the sappers that two platoons of the Pontefract Pioneers are the very men for this particular work. We are the skilled artisans of the infantry, for we go over the top with them to consolidate the positions they capture, and occasionally – though the performance is strictly forbidden – take joyous part in the actual hand-to-hand fighting. Apart from that, we construct machine-gun emplacements for them, dig their communication and jumping-off trenches, help them with their wiring and make ourselves generally useful. We work in front of the front line and we work at the back of the back line. Sometimes we work by day and rest by night; at others we work by night and rest by day. Usually, however, we work by day and get put on a fresh job at night. We are the fairy godmothers of the artillery. We make fascine, plank, and corduroy roads by which they get their guns into position. We construct light railways to bring up their ammunition and make mule tracks for the same purpose. We dig cable trenches through heavily shelled areas that they may be in telephonic communication with their O. Pips.

Our ranks are filled from every trade and profession in and out of the Directory. Our work varies from putting a new washer on the General's pump to constructing elephant shelters in the back areas for conscientious objectors.

'Pioneers .... pioneers,' mused a red-hatted Staff Captain to me the other day. 'Sort of labour battalion, aren't you?' 'We sure are', I agreed.

Appendix II

Despatches

During the course of the war the 31st Division was mentioned many times in Dispatches and in newspaper accounts of the fighting. In the body of this work several quotations from such sources have been made. It is, however, impracticable to include every mention but it is considered desirable to quote the following passages taken from a pamphlet printed by the Divisional Headquarters Staff.

The narratives relate in every case to the fighting during the great German offensive of March–April, 1918.

1. FIRST DISPATCH.
For dogged and courageous fighting, refusing to retire and saving the line on March 3rd and following days. (Details unfortunately not available).

2. SECOND DISPATCH (April 23rd 1918).
Amongst the Divisions which gloriously distinguished themselves in the German onrush is specially mentioned to-day the 31st.

The following telegraphic dispatch has been received today from General Headquarters in France and is issued by the Press Bureau :

The number of divisions employed by the enemy against the British alone since the opening of his offensive on March 21st already is 102, and many of these have been employed twice or thrice. In resisting the heavy blows which such a concentration of troops has enabled the enemy to direct against the British Army, all ranks, arms, and services have behaved with a gallantry, courage, and resolution for which no praise can be too high. Mention has been made in previous communiqués of certain British divisions for conduct of outstanding gallantry. Many other divisions also have greatly distinguished themselves. The Guards Division, after five days of heavy fighting at Boiry-Becquekelle, completely repulsed hostile attacks delivered in great strength on March 28th, and again on March 30th inflicting heavy losses on the enemy. This division, with the 31st and 3rd Divisions on its right and left, in severe fighting on those and other occasions, successfully resisted all the enemy's efforts to open out the northern flank of his attack.

Appendix III

Battle Honours Awarded

The Battle Honours awarded by the War Office to the King's Own Yorkshire
Light Infantry (twenty-six Battalions) are as follows:

MONS: LE CATEAU: MARNE, 1914-18: AISNE, 1914-18: LA BASSÉE.
1914: MESSINES, 1914-17-18: YPRES, 1914-15-17-18: HILL 60,
GRAVENSTAFEL: ST. JULIEN: FREZENBERGH: BELLEWAARDE:
HOOGE, 1915: LOOS: SOMME, 1916-18: ALBERT, 1916-18:
BAZENTIN: DELVILLE WOOD: POZIÈRES: GUILLEMONT:
FLERS-COURCELETTE: MORVAL: LE TRANSLOY: ANCRE, 1916:
ARRAS, 1917-18: SCARPE, 1917: LANGEMARCK, 1917: MENIN
ROAD: POLYGON WOOD: BROODSEINDE: POELCAPPELLE:
PASCHENDAELE: CAMBRAI, 17-18: ST. QUENTIN: BAPAUME,1918:
LYS: HAZEBROUK: BAILLIEUL: KEMMEL: SCHERPENBERG:
TARDENOIS: AMIENS: HINDENBURG LINE: HAVRINCOURT:
ÉPEHY: CANAL DU NORD: ST. QUENTIN CANAL: BEAUVOIS:
SELLE: VALENCIENNES: SAMBRE: FRANCE AND FLANDERS,
1914-18: PIAVE: VITTORIO VENETO, ITALY, 1917-18. MACEDONIA,
1915-17: EGYPT, 1915-16.

Index

GENERAL INDEX